FREESTYLE SPARRING

Grandmaster Woo Jin Jung
with
Jennifer Lawler, PhD

Library of Congress Cataloging-in-Publication Data

Jung, Woo Jin, 1943-
    Freestyle sparring / Woo Jin Jung with Jennifer Lawler.
        p.   cm.
    Includes bibliographical references (p.) and index
    ISBN 0-7360-0129-8
    1. Martial arts--Training.   2. Tae kwon do--Training.   3. Karate-
-Training.   I. Lawler, Jennifer, 1965-   . II. Title.
GV1102.7.T7J86 2000
796.8--dc21

99-36249
CIP

ISBN: 0-7360-0129-8

Acquisitions Editor: Jeff Riley; **Developmental Editor:** Laura Hambly; **Assistant Editor:** Stephan Seyfert; **Copyeditor:** Patsy Fortney; **Proofreader:** Jim Burns; **Indexer:** Daniel Connolly; **Graphic Designer:** Nancy Rasmus; **Graphic Artist:** Dody Bullerman; **Cover Designer:** Jack W. Davis; **Photographer (cover):** ©1999 Medley of Photography/Berry Medley; **Photographer (interior):** Tom Roberts, unless otherwise noted. Photo on p. 1©Ray Malace, p. 51© SportCam USA, and p. 109 © Berry Medley/Medley of Photography; **Illustrator:** Accurate Art Inc.; **Printer:** Versa Press

Human Kinetics books are available at special discounts for bulk purchase. Special editions or book excerpts can also be created to specification. For details, contact the Special Sales Manager at Human Kinetics.

Printed in the United States of America   10 9 8 7 6 5 4 3 2 1

Human Kinetics
Web site: http://www.humankinetics.com

United States: Human Kinetics
P.O. Box 5076
Champaign, IL 61825-5076
1-800-747-4457
e-mail: humank@hkusa.com

Canada: Human Kinetics
475 Devonshire Road Unit 100
Windsor, ON N8Y 2:L5
1-800-465-7301 (in Canada only)
e-mail: humank@hkcanada.com

Europe: Human Kinetics, P.O. Box IW14
Leeds LS16 6TR, United Kingdom
+44 (0) 113-278 1708
e-mail: humank@hkeurope.com

Australia: Human Kinetics
57A Price Avenue
Lower Mitcham, South Australia 5062
(08) 82771555
e-mail: humank@hkaustralia.com

New Zealand: Human Kinetics
P.O. Box 105-231, Auckland Central
09-523-3462
e-mail: humank@hknewz.com

I dedicate this book to my family for their love, loyalty, and support.

Master Woo Jin Jung

This book is dedicated to my husband, Bret Kay, for the usual reasons.

Jennifer Lawler

CONTENTS

PREFACE

Martial artists benefit from freestyle sparring in many ways. Because it takes considerable energy to spar nonstop for several two-minute rounds, it improves physical condition and endurance. Sparring improves martial arts techniques, making them faster and more accurate. It also increases the martial artist's sense of timing. After you've sparred a while, you can spot an opening and strike without even thinking about it. All of these factors are important should a self-defense situation ever arise—and many martial artists say this is one of the main reasons they practice martial arts. Finally, practicing freestyle sparring makes one a better martial artist by improving discipline, self-control, and concentration.

Some people enjoy freestyle sparring as one aspect of martial arts training, realizing that it hones their skills and improves their techniques. For these martial artists, that's more than enough. Others, however, want to pit their skills against other martial artists. They want to compete. Martial artists in either category will find their needs met with this book, which describes the ins and outs of freestyle sparring, both in practice and in competition, for all martial artists, especially those who practice either of the two most popular styles, Karate and Taekwondo.

Whatever stage you're in—beginning to advanced—this book will help you get to the next level. It is the ultimate freestyle sparring resource, covering the physical and mental aspects of practice and competition for all levels. Even if you're already an advanced fighter, you'll find some ideas for spicing up your sparring, adding variety to your arsenal, and improving your physical condition. For those of you at beginning and intermediate stages, there's plenty of information on improving techniques, working on timing, and planning sparring strategies.

The proper techniques and sequences used in sparring are fully illustrated. This, in addition to the complete workout programs, will take the guesswork out of your training.

Freestyle Sparring is divided into three parts. The first part focuses on the art of Taekwondo while the second part concentrates on Karate. Both Karate and

Taekwondo practitioners will find valuable information in the third section, which covers everything from mental and physical readiness to sample workout programs. In short, there's something for everyone. Because of the influence of Taekwondo and Karate on most sparring techniques, this book will be of interest to practitioners of *all* sparring styles.

Chapter 1 primes you for sparring; it covers everything from uniforms and protective gear to the rules and regulations of Taekwondo practice and competition. Chapter 2 gets to the heart of sparring, the techniques. Hand and kicking techniques are covered as well as defensive maneuvers. The punches, kicks, and blocks in this chapter run the gamut from the basics to much more advanced techniques. Each technique is fully illustrated with a photo or a series of photos to show proper form. In chapter 3, "Taekwondo Tactics," you'll learn how to put these techniques to work. Attacking/defending sequences are presented for practice with a partner, heavy bag, or shadow sparring. You'll also get tips on finding a style of fighting that works best for you.

Part II, chapters 4 through 6, covers the same subject matter, yet focuses on Karate. Karate practitioners will benefit from the many techniques and strategies these chapters offer.

A martial artist may have great talent and be able to execute flawless physical techniques, but without *kokoro* (heart or spirit), failure is imminent. Chapter 7 describes ways to achieve and maintain *kokoro,* as well as increase focus and concentration, achieve balance, and boost confidence. Cultivating the right mental attitude is vital to improving your martial arts skills.

Also essential to sharpening your skills is a high level of fitness. Chapter 8 provides you with tips for developing and maintaining the body conditioning you need to spar well, including speed and strength training, flexibility exercises, and explosive power drills that you can add to your workouts for optimum sparring performance.

In sparring, timing is crucial. You can learn to anticipate openings and counterattack more quickly and smoothly with the timing drills in chapter 9. Once you've got the timing down, you can continue to improve your sparring by incorporating techniques from other fighting arts into your arsenal. Chapter 10 describes ways to add new ideas and strategies to your sparring. Finally, hone your skills and become the best fighter possible by following the complete workout programs in chapter 11.

As soon as a martial artist decides there's nothing left to learn, he or she stagnates and becomes easy to defeat. Therefore, use the skills, strategies, and conditioning in *Freestyle Sparring* to build your sparring arsenal. Polish your skills with practice and, like a true warrior, learn to fight with power, speed, strength, wisdom, and intelligence. Always be on the lookout for new ideas and learning opportunities. Most important, never give up. Martial artists with indomitable spirit are truly victorious.

ACKNOWLEDGMENTS

We would like to thank all of those individuals who helped make this book possible. We extend our appreciation to Master Donald Booth, who did a wonderful job of working with us as interpreter, adviser, and loyal supporter. We also appreciate the ideas and insights of Master Susan Booth. Special thanks goes to Mr. Chris Frailey, technical adviser for the Karate section. J.P. Merz is also owed a debt of gratitude for the fine drawings he created. We also thank the models who appear in this book: Guy Smith, Gail Kinzler, Bret Kay, Hyungho Choi, and Christine Brewer.

I would like to thank all of the students who have enriched my life so much over the years, and the community of Cedar Rapids, Iowa, for welcoming me and my school all those years ago. Special recognition goes to the black belts and instructors who have contributed so much of their time and talent to making my school one to be proud of.

Master Woo Jin Jung

I would like to express my appreciation for the black belts at New Horizons in Lawrence, Kansas, and for those at Jung's Academy in Cedar Rapids, Iowa, who have so kindly spent many hours answering questions and posing for photographs. Thanks also to my husband, the finest martial artist I have ever met and an all-around good guy, for never minding about the little things; to my delightful daughter, Jessica, for showing me what perseverance really is; and to my parents, Tom and Yvonne Lawler, who just happened to be around whenever I needed them.

Jennifer Lawler

PART I

TAEKWONDO SPARRING

CHAPTER 1
TAEKWONDO ESSENTIALS

The essence of sparring is in knowing the self. Practicing Taekwondo leads to an awareness of one's inward effort and promotes self-discipline and self-control.

Most martial artists who wish to improve their sparring skills are already enrolled in classes at a formal martial arts school. If this is the case for you, remember to always take into account everything your instructor tells you. For example, your instructor may not allow hand techniques to the head during practice sparring. If this is the case, respect your instructor and don't use such techniques. If your instructor has suggestions for improving your sparring, incorporate them as well. Take what you can from the information available to you. By applying the principles that make sense to you, you will become a better martial artist.

Also remember that sparring is only one aspect of the martial arts experience. Don't neglect other areas—forms, techniques practice—to focus only on sparring. Doing so makes you just another fighter, not a martial artist. Martial artists are supposed to develop character as well as physical skills. Don't forget this essential focus of martial arts training.

This chapter shows you how to select and find appropriate clothing and equipment, describes the basic rules of Taekwondo sparring, and provides information on tournament competition.

Clothing and Equipment

The proper clothing and equipment not only help cushion blows, but also can prevent more serious injury to you and your partner. Invest in clothing and equipment that are appropriate to your style of sparring, whether it be heavy contact, light contact, or no contact.

Workout Clothes

Whenever you practice any aspect of the martial arts, wear appropriate workout clothing. Many martial artists prefer to work out in traditional uniforms. They feel that taking their street clothes off and putting the uniform on reminds them of their connection and obligations to the martial arts. A martial artist must always represent his or her art and school with character, honesty, and effort. Dishonoring the uniform by practicing in a lazy way or by failing to respect your training partners is a serious offense to traditional martial artists. They feel that wearing the uniform reminds them to work well and to work hard. Putting the uniform on puts them in the right frame of mind for practicing with intensity and focus.

Other martial artists feel differently. When they work out, they want to be comfortable. They are less concerned about maintaining a traditional attitude toward the martial arts and want to work out in what feels good to them. In either case, there are some guidelines to remember.

1. Clothing should not be restrictive. You should be able to move freely so that your kicks and punches flow naturally. The only exception is when you work on self-defense scenarios. In this case, martial artists will sometimes practice sparring techniques in their regular clothes in order to discover what techniques work under what conditions. For example, a man in a suit and tie might find it hard to execute a spinning wheel kick. A woman in a skirt might find a reverse kick out of the question. By practicing techniques in street clothes, martial artists can learn what will work in a self-defense situation. But this, of course, is not a typical workout.

2. If you choose to wear a sweatsuit or shorts and a T-shirt, be certain to keep your shirt tucked in. If your clothing gets caught on your competitor's hand or foot, one or both of you could be injured (and you could be out a shirt).

3. If you decide to wear a traditional uniform, make certain the top stays closed at all times. Some Taekwondo uniforms have a tunic-type top that doesn't come open. Other Taekwondo uniforms have wrap-type tops. These may require special attention. Occasionally a safety pin inserted in a strategic place will prevent the top from coming open and catching on the opponent's hand or foot. Some martial artists wear a T-shirt tucked into uniform pants, tied with their rank belt, when they practice sparring. This can be a good compromise.

4. Never wear makeup or jewelry while sparring. Makeup runs, gets in your eyes, and stains clothing. Although it isn't dangerous, it isn't appropriate. Jewelry, on the other hand, can be dangerous. Jewelry can scratch your partner and can catch in your (or your partner's) clothing. Remember to remove necklaces, rings, and earrings before working out. In addition, glasses should not be worn during sparring practice. Use contact lenses instead, or invest in safety glasses designed specifically for sports.

Protective Gear

It is prudent to invest in protective gear (also called sparring equipment or sparring gear). Sparring gear simply consists of padded protectors that keep you and your partner from getting bruised, especially if you accidentally kick too hard or if you happen to block an elbow instead of a hand. Because it actually protects your partner more than it protects you, you should insist that your partner wear sparring gear too. This is especially important if you spar with medium or heavy contact.

There are a number of pieces of sparring equipment that you can use to protect yourself and others, and what you decide to equip yourself with depends on what your sparring is like (no contact? heavy contact?), what your regular partners do, and what your instructor, if any, recommends.

Headgear

Headgear, like a helmet, protects the sides and back of your head from kicks and punches. Headgear can be purchased with a masklike face protector so that a kick to the face doesn't break the nose. The drawback is that the bigger, more complicated, and heavier your headgear, the harder it is to see what you're doing. For this reason, headgear can be a bit of a handicap, at least until you are comfortable with it. But protecting your head is essential since Taekwondo fighters frequently kick to the head.

Mouthguard

The mouthguard is another essential item. It protects the teeth from jarring blows that can crack or loosen teeth or cause other dental problems. Mouthguards are sold in several sizes for adults and children. They are usually boiled in water until pliable, then fitted to the mouth and allowed to cool. This ensures a custom fit. Mouthguards are an extremely inexpensive way to save your teeth.

Chest Protector

In some styles of Taekwondo, such as WTF (World Taekwondo Federation) style or Olympic style, chest protectors are mandatory for sparring. At WTF-sponsored tournaments, you will be required to wear one. If you spar with fairly heavy contact, a chest protector can be a wise investment. Some martial artists, however, find them cumbersome and feel they inhibit their kicks and body movement. If you spar with light contact and are associated with a non-WTF school, or spar in non-WTF competition, skip the chest protector.

Groin Protector

If you're a man, you need one of these. No sparring in tournaments is allowed without one, and as anyone who has tried it will tell you, you don't want to practice sparring without one. Groin protectors are also available for women, but most women who've tried them say they are uncomfortable and unnecessary. Some physicians have even speculated that using female groin protectors can cause more harm than going without, although most such evidence is anecdotal, not scientific.

Forearm Guards

Forearm guards protect the forearms from the bumps and bruises that occur when one blocks kicks and punches. Although some people swear by them, others feel they are not very worthwhile. Most Taekwondo practitioners find they can live without forearm guards, but some discover that they get too many arm bruises if they don't wear them. Spar for a while before making a decision one way or another. WTF-style competition requires forearm guards.

Hand Protectors

Hand or fist protectors are also called "punches" because that's what they protect against. Fighters who use a lot of hand techniques should purchase hand protectors not just for their own sake but for the protection of their partners. If a hand technique goes a little hard or gets a little out of control, the hand protector will help cushion the blow.

There are several kinds of hand protectors. The most common covers the whole hand and straps around the wrist. They are either padded cotton or plastic-covered foam. Most beginning and intermediate martial artists use these protectors quite comfortably. An alternative is a glove-style hand protector, which looks like a padded, fingerless glove. These are usually made of leather. This style is sometimes used by advanced practitioners, especially if they also do bag work and if they use open hand techniques in their sparring. This type may not be accepted at tournaments, so be sure to have backup hand protectors.

Shin Guards

Shin guards protect the shins from bumps and bruises. As with the forearm guard, some martial artists don't need them at all, while others swear by them. Whether you need them depends on your sparring style. If you spar hard, you should probably wear them. If you use your legs a lot to block kicks, protect your midsection, and deliver strikes, you may find yourself with plenty of shin bruises, so you should go ahead and use them. Again, try sparring for a bit before investing in shin guards. WTF-style competition requires shin guards.

Foot Protectors

Foot protectors are sometimes called "kicks" because that's what they protect against. Taekwondo fighters should wear kicks when sparring to protect their partners. It is easy for a person to accidentally kick too hard or inaccurately.

There are several types of foot protectors. One type slides onto the foot, protecting the top or instep of the foot. Another type is a combination foot protector/shin guard. It is all one piece and it slides over the top of the foot and covers the shin. Both of these are preferred by WTF-style or Olympic-style Taekwondo practitioners. They protect well against roundhouse kicks (which use the top of the foot as the striking surface). The drawback is that they don't protect the heel or the bottom of the foot at all. If you perform kicks that use the heel as the striking surface, such as axe kicks and spinning wheel kicks, your partner won't be protected should you accidentally strike too hard.

Another type of foot protector covers the entire foot, including the toes and the sides of the feet. It attaches with a strap that goes around the foot. This type is preferred by martial artists who perform kicks that use the heel as the striking surface. Its only drawback is that it is slightly heavier and more cumbersome than the other types.

Headgear

Hand protectors

Chest protector

Shin guards

Foot protectors

Taekwondo sparring equipment.

Where to Find Uniforms and Equipment

If you plan to enter formal competition, you will need to be outfitted with the appropriate uniform and gear. If you plan to participate in WTF-sanctioned events (most national and international tournaments are this style), make certain any uniform you purchase is WTF-approved. You will also be required to wear shin and forearm guards, a groin protector (if you're a man), headgear, a mouthguard, and a chest protector (which is sometimes provided by the tournament organizer; check ahead of time).

If you are taking formal lessons from an instructor, he or she can often provide uniforms and sparring gear at a reasonable cost. If not, many larger sporting goods stores carry various lines of martial arts equipment. Some larger cities have martial arts supply stores (these merit a visit even if you don't need sparring equipment). You can also purchase martial arts equipment through the following mail-order houses, which will be happy to send catalogs at your request:

American Martial Arts Supply
5848 East Speedway Boulevard
Tucson, AZ 85712
Telephone: 800-283-1299
520-740-0479
www.amas.net

Macho Products, Inc.
10045 102nd Terrace
Sebastian, FL 32958
Telephone: 800-327-6812
561-388-9892
www.macho.com

Century Martial Arts Supply, Inc.
1705 National Boulevard
Midwest City, OK 73110
Telephone: 800-626-2787
405-732-2226
www.centuryma.com

Pil Sung Martial Arts Supply, LLC.
6300 Ridglea Place, Suite 1008
Fort Worth, TX 76116
Telephone: 800-992-0388
817-738-5408
www.pil-sung.com

Practice Matches

Practice sparring matches can have as many rules or as few rules as you and your partners agree on. Sometimes when Taekwondo fighters are practicing, they will agree that takedown or throwing techniques are acceptable. This helps them to realize what might happen in a street fight and is a more realistic approach to sparring than is usually taken.

For the most part, however, practice sparring follows set rules. The legal target areas include

- the chest (including the sides),
- the shoulders,
- the sides of the head, and
- the face.

In other words, everything above the belt is a legal target area with the following exceptions. Illegal target areas include

- the neck,
- the back of the head,
- the back,
- the legs, and
- the groin.

In practice sparring, all kicking techniques are legal to all target areas. No knee strikes are allowed. Straight punches are often restricted to the chest area only. (It is very easy for a straight punch to the high section to end up breaking someone's nose.) Backfists and spinning backfists to the high section are sometimes allowed. Advanced practitioners are frequently allowed to use open hand techniques, such as knife hand strikes and ridge hand strikes, to all target areas.

The amount of contact allowed can vary, depending on the partners. No contact is often the rule for beginners, light-to-medium contact for intermediate practitioners, and medium-to-heavy contact for advanced fighters.

Remember that freestyle sparring can be dangerous, so use caution at all times. If your partner asks you to back your intensity level down, respect your partner's wishes. Use good control at all times and agree with your partner ahead of time regarding how much contact is acceptable (no contact, light contact, medium contact, heavy contact—and agree on what these terms mean!). Although no one who spars does so without acquiring at least a couple of bruises every now and then, remember that a good freestyle fighter doesn't need to pound on his or her partner. One sign of true talent is the ability to score points and make contact with one's partner without leaving bruises behind. Excellent control is the hallmark of an exceptional martial artist.

Sparring is usually held in continuous rounds (no stopping) for one or two minutes at a time. Practice sessions can last as long as the partners wish. Points scored are usually not kept; if they are, it is most frequently done by an informal acknowledgment system in which each partner acknowledges when a legal technique has landed, unblocked, to a legal target area. This is usually done by a nod of the head or a quick, "good point."

Competition

Taekwondo sparring differs from tournament to tournament. National and international events usually abide by WTF rules, but local and regional competitions may not. Therefore, always check with the tournament sponsor or check the tournament rules sheet before attending a tournament competition. Check the rules well ahead of time so you can adjust your practice sparring to reflect the tournament rules. For instance, if you are accustomed to using backfists to the temple when sparring and the tournament you are planning to attend doesn't allow this, you should practice sparring without the backfist so you don't accidentally use it in competition.

National and International Tournaments

WTF-sanctioned (also called Olympic-style) competition is the most common of national and international Taekwondo tournaments. However, since tournament rules vary depending on the sponsoring organization, check ahead of time. In WTF-style tournaments, sparring competitors must wear a WTF-approved Taekwondo uniform (always white; although blue satin may look nice on television, it's not allowed). When purchasing a uniform, check to be certain it is WTF-approved. WTF competitors must also wear shin and forearm guards, a groin protector (if you're a man), headgear, a mouthguard, and a chest protector. Fighters are not allowed to spar in competition without this equipment.

Protocol

The referee or head judge calls the competitors to the ring. They bow to him or her, then to each other to show courtesy and good sportsmanship. The referee tells them to assume fighting stances. He or she then gives the command to begin. At the end of each round, competitors bow to each other, and at the end of the match they bow to each other, the referee, and the judges.

Tournament Divisions

Competitors are matched by belt rank, age, gender, and size. Most Taekwondo tournaments have a variety of different divisions, but at some of the smaller tournaments, you may be matched with people from a variety of ranks and sizes. If there are enough competitors, they will be divided into weight classes, such as light, medium, and heavy weight. Adults are sometimes further divided by age; a senior division might include competitors over 35. More divisions are often made in the black belt category. There may be additional weight classes and divisions according to the *dan* (degree) of black belt. In international competition, there are 8 recognized weight classes for adults and 10 for junior fighters (those aged 15 to 18). The difference in each of these weight classes is about 10 pounds.

Length of Matches

Sparring matches usually consist of three rounds, each lasting three minutes, with a one-minute rest between rounds. An official scorekeeper keeps track of time. Sparring is continuous and is only stopped if a foul occurs or one fighter steps out of the ring.

Ring Size

The ring is actually a square. Officially it measures 8 meters by 8 meters (about 26 feet by 26 feet), although in practice this will sometimes vary. A 12-meter by 12-meter (about 39 feet by 39 feet) out-of-bounds marker is placed farther out. Competitors are expected to stay within the 8 × 8-meter ring.

Judges

A referee or head judge directs the action, signals fighters to begin, and enforces safety and discipline. Four corner judges watch the action and score the match. If the four judges disagree about who is the winner, the referee makes the decision. Two jurors watch the match to catch mistakes the referee or judges might make.

Head and face

Shoulders

Chest above the belt

Sides

Legal target areas in Taekwondo sparring.

Legal Target Areas

Legal target areas for WTF tournament sparring include the chest above the belt, including the sides and the shoulders, plus the face and the sides of the head. The back of the head is never a legal target area. The back is not a legal target area, and nothing below the belt is legal.

Scoring Points

In WTF competition, only kicks and closed hand techniques score points. Open hand techniques, such as knife hand and ridge hand, are not allowed. Knee strikes are also not allowed. While hand techniques to the head are not allowed, kicks to the head are. If you land an unblocked kick or punch to a legal target area so that it results in a "trembling shock," you will earn a point. A "trembling shock" visibly moves the opponent through space. This means the opponent steps back or is pushed back by the blow. If you fall down or grab your opponent to keep your balance when striking, the point does not score. Scoring a knockout kick to the head results in a win, although strikes to the neck and punches to the head are prohibited. Sparring goes on continuously and judges award points as they see them, without stopping the contestants. If fouls occur, points are deducted from the perpetrator's total.

If the point total is equal after the three-round match, the referee selects the winner based on which competitor used superior techniques. If this is impossible to determine, or if the techniques are equal, the referee gives the match to the competitor who proved more aggressive. If all of the above are equal, the fighter with the best sportsmanship and etiquette will be awarded the match.

Techniques Scale

- A technique that results in an eight-count knockdown (or knockout) is superior to all others.
- A kick is superior to a hand technique.
- A jumping technique is superior to a standing technique.
- A kick to the head is superior to a kick to the body.
- A counterattack is superior to an offensive attack.

Rules Infractions

Warnings are given for certain rules infractions or fouls. These warnings are called *kyong-go*. For every two warnings a competitor receives during a round, an entire point is deducted from his or her score. Some rules infractions, such as attacking a fallen opponent, result in an immediate one-point deduction. These are *gam-jeum* penalties. If a competitor has three points deducted from his or her score, he or she loses the match. Warnings and point deductions are determined and enforced by the head referee, although the corner judges may also point them out.

Penalties

Kyong-go (half-point) penalties

- Punching to the face
- Pushing the opponent down with a foot
- Intentionally falling to the floor, especially to evade a strike
- Pushing the opponent with the hands, shoulder, or body
- Pretending pain or injury
- Interfering with the course of the contest
- Stepping out of the 8 × 8-meter ring, either forced or on purpose
- Grabbing the opponent or his or her uniform
- Using a knee strike
- Turning away to avoid a strike
- Striking to a nontarget area, including the legs and the groin
- Throwing, sweeping, or otherwise taking down the opponent
- Attempting to convince the judges a point was scored
- Offensive language or unsportsmanlike conduct

Gam-jeum (full-point) penalties

- Continuing to attack the opponent after the referee has stopped the round or declared "break"
- Any headbutt against the opponent
- Attacking a fallen opponent
- Causing injury with a hand technique to the face
- Stepping out of the 12 × 12-meter out-of-bounds marker
- Striking the back or the back of the head on purpose
- Serious disregard for proper conduct; serious breach of etiquette

Local and Regional Tournaments

No matter what the Olympic committee would have you believe, there are other types of Taekwondo competition besides WTF-sanctioned events. These are usually local or regional events sponsored by specific Taekwondo schools or clubs. Often they are by invitation only—you must belong to a formal school in the area in order to attend. Sometimes, however, tournaments are open, meaning you simply need a clean uniform to enter.

Local and regional tournaments are often a good way to get started in competition. They tend to be less intimidating. There are fewer competitors, so the likelihood of doing well is increased, which can improve one's confidence. Also, they do not require the same investment of time and money. Often your instructor can recommend good local and regional tournaments. He or she may know which ones are likely to be well organized and well run. Once you've had some success at this level, you may wish to move on to national or international competition, and that often means WTF-sanctioned events.

Tournament Divisions

In local and regional tournaments, the tournament organizers determine the sparring rules. Usually the fighting divisions are broader because there are fewer competitors. For example, all blue belt men might find themselves sparring in the same division. Black belt men might only be divided into three weight categories: light, medium, and heavy. Since fewer women compete, lower belt women might find themselves competing with a variety of ranks, such as yellow, orange, and green in one division. Therefore, it pays to be flexible when participating in local and regional tournaments.

Length of Matches

Local and regional tournaments are also less uniform regarding match length and ring size. Match length is usually only one round of two or three minutes. Thus, you must be prepared to move quickly and aggressively to score. At black belt level, this is often increased to two rounds of two minutes each, with a one-minute rest between rounds. These tournaments frequently have a "Grand Champion" match, open only to black belts, in which winners of the various black belt divisions spar each other to determine who is the best fighter among all competitors. This match is usually a two-round match, with two-minute rounds, and a one-minute rest between. Certain national and international competitions also have a "Grand Champion" match.

Ring Size

Although an 8-meter by 8-meter (about 26 feet by 26 feet) ring is ideal, smaller rings are often used in these smaller competitions. Sparring in a smaller ring requires practice to keep from stepping out of the ring. Consult with martial artists who have attended the tournament in the past to learn about such idiosyncrasies.

Judges

At local and regional tournaments, the organizers often depend on black belts who are participating in the tournament to help judge the tournament. This means that judges have a wide range of experience. This also limits the number of judges that are assigned to any one ring. In such competitions, it is not unusual for a referee and four corner judges to make up the entire judging committee. Jurors are usually not used. Sometimes a timekeeper who doubles as a scorekeeper is used to oversee the competition and make sure no mistakes are made.

The amount of contact that is allowed also varies. In WTF-sanctioned competition, a "trembling shock" must occur for a point to be awarded. That requires fairly heavy contact. In many local and regional tournaments, the organizers prefer to see better control and will specify light contact or uniform-only contact. This requires better technique and control, but it also means that points are less obvious and aren't always spotted. This can prove frustrating for competitors who feel they are scoring points that simply aren't being seen.

Legal Target Areas

Legal target areas and legal techniques also vary. Usually the sides of the head and the chest, including the sides, are legal target areas. Local and regional tournament organizers often restrict or ban kicks or strikes to the face, because this can cause injury. Hand techniques are usually allowed only to the chest area. Usually only closed hand techniques (punches, backfists) are allowed, but sometimes black belts may use open hands, such as knife hands and ridge hands. All of these rules should be listed on the tournament rules sheet provided by the tournament sponsor.

Scoring Points

In local and regional tournaments, points can be awarded following the WTF- or Olympic-style format, in which the rounds are continuous and the judges keep track of points on a score sheet. Often, however, the more traditional, Japanese-inspired point-scoring system is used, in which competitors do not spar continuously. In this case, the competitors begin sparring and as soon as the referee or any of the four corner judges sees an unblocked legal strike to a legal target area, he or she calls, "Point!" The referee stops the fight, asks the judges to score, and counts the number of judges who agree that a point has been scored. The referee will add his or her opinion. If a majority of scorers (judges and referee) agrees that a point has been scored, a point is awarded and the timekeeper, who doubles as a scorekeeper, makes a note of the point. The referee then returns the fighters to the starting position and starts the match again. Sometimes the clock runs even during stoppage of action. At other times the clock is stopped while points are awarded.

Using this system, one point is awarded for a punch or kick to the middle section (the chest area) and two points are awarded for a kick to the high section (the head). A trembling shock need not be applied. The criterion for a point is simply this: a well-executed technique must land, unblocked, to a legal target area. Warnings and point deductions are given for rules infractions similar to WTF-sanctioned competitions. In point-scoring competitions, however, sometimes only one or two warnings are required before a competitor is disqualified. In these competitions, if blood is ever drawn, the attacker is disqualified.

The point-scoring system, with its stoppage of action, requires special practice on the part of the fighter. Fighters who rely primarily on defensive or counterattacking techniques will find themselves at a disadvantage in this kind of tournament, because their opponent might land a point (thus causing stoppage of play) before they can respond with a counterattack. Therefore, fighters who initiate attacks or are more offense-minded tend to do better.

Because of these variations, be aware of what type of tournament you are planning to enter, get a list of the rules, and practice sparring according to the organizer's planned rules.

Rules Infractions

At local and regional tournaments, fouls are called for illegal techniques (such as knee strikes), attacks to an illegal target area, stepping out of bounds, turning one's back on the opponent, and drawing blood. Other fouls may also be called. The organizers will announce these, plus penalties, ahead of time. Use the WTF list of fouls in order to practice clean tournament sparring. (See page 11.)

By planning ahead and knowing the rules, you can organize your practice sessions so that you will compete at your best level. Even if you do not plan to compete, understanding sparring rules helps you become a more effective fighter. Lack of preparation can lead to failure—and not just in the sparring ring. Knowing the essentials of Taekwondo sparring can improve your overall martial arts abilities and skills.

CHAPTER 2

TAEKWONDO TECHNIQUES

Sparring assists one in becoming a person of action, which is preferable to the theorist.

In order to succeed in sparring, you must execute Taekwondo techniques correctly. You must also know when to use different techniques. By understanding the purpose of each block or strike, your overall sparring strategy will improve. Also, by practicing sparring techniques repeatedly, you will become faster and more powerful—a potent combination in a fighter! For these reasons, even if you are well skilled in basic Taekwondo techniques, take the time to learn how and when to use different techniques. This chapter will show you the ropes.

Legal Techniques

Although Taekwondo practitioners have many different techniques at their disposal, only a select number of these are allowed in freestyle sparring competition. For example, although a palm strike to the face could stop an attacker, it's never allowed in competitive sparring. Although you may practice with whatever techniques you and your partners mutually agree on, if you plan to spar in tournament competition, you should practice using only those techniques that are allowed in competition—that is, "legal techniques."

Although some competitions allow black belt competitors to use the backfist to the head or to use open hand techniques to all target areas, unless you know for certain that the competition you are preparing for allows such techniques, it is best to practice as if they were not allowed.

In Taekwondo competition, closed hand techniques are allowed to the middle section. This includes the backfist and the punch. (In WTF competitions, the backfist is not allowed.) Practice sparring using only closed hand techniques.

Knee strikes are not allowed. Of the kicking techniques, the front kick, side kick, roundhouse kick, reverse (or back) kick, hooking kick, and crescent or axe kick are all sound, legal techniques for sparring matches. More advanced fighters can add spinning wheel kicks, reverse crescent kicks, and others to their arsenals, but these are not necessary at first.

Legal Versus Illegal Techniques for Taekwondo Sparring Matches

Legal Techniques

Closed Hand Techniques
   Backfist*
   Punch**
Kicking Techniques
   Front kick
   Side kick
   Roundhouse kick
   Reverse (or back) kick
   Hooking kick
   Crescent (or axe) kick
   Spinning wheel kick
   Reverse crescent (or axe) kick
   Jumping kick

Illegal Techniques

Knee strikes
Open hand techniques
Takedown or throwing techniques

*The backfist is not allowed in WTF competitions.

**The backfist and punch are usually allowed only to the middle section or chest area.

Stances

When fighters begin a sparring match, they usually face each other, assume an attention stance, bow (as a courtesy), and then assume a fighting stance before beginning the round.

ATTENTION STANCE

The attention stance should be solid and strong. Both feet should be together, and arms should be at your sides. Look straight ahead. From this position, you will bow to your partner.

READY STANCE

After the bow, assume the ready stance, which is done by placing your feet shoulder-width apart and bringing your arms forward, hands as fists, in front of your solar plexus or midsection.

FIGHTING STANCE

From the ready stance, step back with either your right leg or your left leg. If you are left handed, you may find it more comfortable to step back with your left leg, and if you are right handed you may wish to step back with your right leg. Some instructors tell their students to always step back with the right leg so that all fighters fight as if right handed; others instruct their students to vary which leg they step back with. The latter is probably the best idea, since it promotes balance and unpredictability.

Your forward foot should point toward your partner and your back foot should be at a 90-degree angle to your front foot. Your chest should be turned away from the front so that you present a smaller target area. Your hands should be in a guarded position, elbows tucked to protect your sides. Keep your weight evenly distributed, but remain light on your feet so that you can strike with a kick at any opportunity.

Kihop or Shout

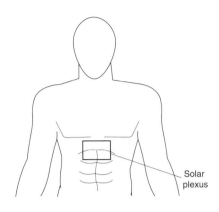

Start the *kihop* by summoning your breath from the solar plexus.

After bowing to your opponent and assuming the fighting stance, the instructor or referee will say, *"sijak!"* or, "begin!" Both fighters then *kihop* or shout before striking. This shows that the fighters are ready for the match to begin. The *kihop* is also used when a strike is delivered to add power and impact to the technique. It is an essential component of the martial artist's sparring arsenal.

The *kihop* helps fighters summon their energy and focus their concentration. Whenever you launch an attack with the intention of scoring a point, a loud *kihop* helps you to focus on your purpose. It also draws the judges' attention so that they are more likely to notice when you score a point. For these reasons, it is important to develop a good *kihop*.

Begin by taking a deep breath. As you slowly exhale, find your solar plexus. It is located between your sternum and your navel. Push in on your solar plexus. This should forcibly expel your breath. Remember that point on your body, and as you summon your breath to *kihop*, start your *kihop* from that point. If you simply use your lungs, you will have a weaker, higher-pitched yell. Also, remember that a scream is not a shout. Young people in particular often make this mistake. Your *kihop* should start deep in your body and focus all of your attention and energy. Good *kihops* during a sparring match can help you win the match.

Hand Techniques

Because Taekwondo is primarily considered a kicking art, judges watch for kicking techniques when scoring a match. Often fighters who punch become frustrated and feel that their punches are being overlooked. It can be difficult for a Taekwondo practitioner to score with a punch rather than a kick, but that doesn't mean punches shouldn't be used. A solid, powerful punch, emphasized by a loud *kihop,* will draw the judges' attention. Also, punches can be used to set up other techniques. For example, a punch to the middle section might draw the opponent's hands down, leaving the head unguarded. Thus, a perfect follow-up to a punch would be a crescent kick to the high section.

Work on developing strong punching skills and you'll find plenty of uses for them in competitive freestyle sparring.

Punches

The backfist is allowed in some sparring tournaments, but since this is rare, it probably should not be used to practice for competition. Instead, the punch (and its variations) is a better bet.

STRAIGHT PUNCH

The straight punch *(chung kwon chigi)* is a fast punch using the front hand. Make a fist by rolling your fingers into a ball and folding your thumb over as a lock. The first two knuckles of your fist make up the striking area. Your wrist and hand should remain

in a straight line. Chamber your arm. The chamber position is different for each technique, but it is essentially the "cocked" or ready position of the technique. From the chamber, the strike travels directly to the target. For the straight punch, your fist should start at your side, slightly above the waist (some martial artists use their belt as a guideline). Pull your arm back and bend your elbow at a 90-degree angle. Your palm should face up. This is the chamber position. Punch forward with your arm. At the end of the strike, twist your wrist so that your palm faces down. This is done to add explosive power to the impact of your punch.

The punch usually extends from slightly above the waist forward, with the power of your shoulder and hips behind it. But to use the technique in sparring, chamber your fist at shoulder level, the way boxers do, to protect your head. Then punch straight out from your shoulder. Thus, the straight punch is similar to a jab. Your nonpunching hand guards your jaw or the middle section.

REVERSE PUNCH

This is a variation of the straight punch. Since it generates more power and is more pronounced, it is easier for judges to see. The reverse punch is performed in exactly the same way as the straight punch. The only difference is the placement of your feet. If you punch with the hand that is on the same side as your front leg, you are throwing a straight punch. If you throw a punch from the same side as your back leg, it is called a reverse punch. You are usually able to generate more power with a reverse punch because of your body position; that is, you can pivot your hips into the punch to get the full force of your entire body behind it. Remember to keep your nonpunching hand in a guarded position to protect your body and your head.

Sparring Tip To get the best effect from the reverse punch, lead with a straight punch. As you pull the straight punch back to protect your head, launch the reverse punch. This often catches the opponent off guard.

Punching Fundamentals

In order to use punching techniques effectively in sparring, you must perform them properly. This requires skills building and repeated practice. Some hints on proper execution and practice drills follow.

Using the Correct Striking Surface

Punching with the correct striking surface is essential. This means that you must hold your wrist straight so that your punching knuckles stay on the same plane as your forearm.

The best way to ensure that you are striking with the first two knuckles of your fist is to use a striking post, which is simply an upright piece of wood, sometimes covered with carpet or other material to prevent cuts, that has been secured to the floor or the ground. By punching the post, you can tell what striking surface you are using on your hand. If a striking post is not available, use any flat surface, such as a wall. (Don't punch with full strength, of course, or you'll end up fixing a hole in the wall.) Practice the punch slowly, extending your arm out until your fist touches the wall. Only the first two knuckles should make contact with the surface. Adjust your fist and the way you hold your hand and arm until you are striking with the correct striking surface.

Martial artists sometimes bend or roll their wrists when they punch. This can cause sprains or tears and reduces the power of the technique. It is a good idea to practice punching a striking post or heavy bag to build your wrist strength. You can also invest in wrist wraps or bag gloves to keep your wrists steady until you've strengthened your wrist and arm muscles sufficiently. An old martial arts exercise for strengthening wrists is to do knuckle push-ups, as described on page 21.

Applying the Chamber and Twist

Two very important concepts to remember about punching are the chamber position and the wrist twist. The chamber position is the ready position of your hand and arm. Make sure your arm is cocked with a strong 90-degree angle. A strong chamber is essential to the correct performance of the technique. The twist at the end of the punch is also extremely important. It helps generate explosive power at the point of impact.

Generating Power

Many martial artists make the mistake of using only their arms to generate power in their punches. They throw only the arm forward, resulting in a less powerful punch. A related problem occurs when martial artists overextend their arms. Sometimes a martial artist tries to add power to a punch or striking technique by throwing the arm so far forward that the shoulder also rolls forward. For best effect, your shoulder should always stay on the same plane as your chest. Don't let your shoulder roll forward beyond your chest.

To generate more power, you don't need to overextend your arm. You do need to put your whole body behind your strike as shown in the photo on page 21. This is done by using your hips to move your body back and forth.

To understand how this works, stand in a front stance. Chamber your fist at your side. As you punch forward, twist the same side hip forward as well. You should notice a sizable difference in the power of your strikes. You can also step or slide into a punch to add power. Practice this by stepping forward and striking at the same time. Combine the step and the hip pivot at the same time to increase the power of your punches significantly.

Using a Punching Bag

It's difficult to measure the power of your punches without using a punching bag, a heavy bag, or another solid target. Use bag gloves or sparring equipment, especially if you haven't been doing much bag work. Try the hip twist and the step

Increase the power of your punches by pivoting your hips forward as you strike.

forward while using the heavy bag to see how they improve your hand striking techniques. To get the most from these suggestions, practice for several minutes on the heavy bag each day. This will also strengthen your arms and wrists to eliminate wrist rolls.

Improving Upper Body Fitness

Upper body strength is essential to explosive punching. Although you can certainly lift weights to become stronger, nothing beats an old-fashioned push-up. Start with very basic push-ups and build up from there. Lie flat on the floor and place your palms directly under your shoulders. Keep your abdomen tight and your body straight, and push up. If these are difficult to do at first, rest your knees on the floor. Your goal, either short or long term depending on your physical condition, should be to perform 75 push-ups in a row, resting only your palms and toes on the floor.

You can vary the push-ups and their physical effects by changing the placement of your hands. By spreading your hands so they are extended two shoulder widths apart, you work more of the chest muscles and biceps. Bringing your hands in close under your sternum works your triceps. Finally, you can do knuckle push-ups. These are done by making your hands into fists and resting your weight on the first two knuckles of each hand (your punching knuckles). Knuckle push-ups strengthen your wrists and forearms to help produce more powerful punches.

If a pull-up bar (sometimes called a chin-up bar) is available, work on pull-ups. If you can't do these at first, have a friend act as spotter. Grip the bar with your hands placed about shoulder-width apart and pull straight up. You can vary the pull-up by changing the grip you have on the bar. A wide grip works the triceps and shoulders. A reverse grip works the biceps.

Punching With Confidence

Because many elements combine to create a powerful punch, you can worry too much about perfect execution. You might worry, is my hand chambered correctly? Am I twisting my palm down at the end? Am I turning my hip into the strike? Then when you strike, you feel tentative, unsure whether you are performing the technique correctly. Always strike with confidence. It may not be a perfect punch, and you may not get your hips pivoted exactly right, but if you have confidence behind your techniques, you'll be a better fighter.

Kicking Techniques

Kicking techniques are those techniques that use any part of the foot as the striking surface. Kicks are most effective when the opponent is several feet away, whereas hand striking techniques are more effective when the opponent is closer.

All kicking techniques can be performed with either the front or back leg. For instance, if you are in a back or fighting stance, you can do a side kick with your forward leg or with your back leg. The only difference is how you shift your weight. A front leg side kick requires you to move your weight to the back leg as you kick, whereas a back leg side kick requires you to move your weight to the front leg. Although front and back leg kicks are basically executed in the same way, they have different purposes. The front leg kick is always faster than the back leg kick, but the back leg kick is always more powerful than the front leg kick. Therefore, which you use will depend on circumstances. The faster kick might distract an opponent, whereas the more powerful kick might score more clearly.

As you learn more about Taekwondo sparring, it will become easier to judge when to use which kick. You will find that some kicks suit your abilities better than others, but all kicks should be practiced since each helps you improve certain aspects of your martial arts training. In competition, you'll more likely use power kicks for WTF-sanctioned events and fast kicks for traditional point-sparring tournaments.

Basic Kicks

Four basic kicks make up the foundation of Taekwondo. These are the front kick, the side kick, the roundhouse kick, and the reverse kick. Most Taekwondo practitioners are introduced to these kicks right away, yet this does not mean they are easy to master or are somehow inferior to more sophisticated or difficult kicks. These kicks will make up as much as 80 percent of your sparring arsenal, so be sure you perform them properly and practice them regularly.

FRONT KICK

The front kick *(ap chaki)* targets an area directly in front of you. In sparring it can be used to strike a middle or high target area. The striking surface is the ball of your foot. Position your foot by pointing your foot and pulling your toes back. To perform the kick, lift your leg high, directly to the front, bending your knee in a 90-degree angle. Snap your leg forward, striking with the ball of your foot.

The front kick can emphasize different movements. The snap front kick is performed with a sharp whipping movement and has the advantage of speed. The push or thrust front kick is performed by pushing the target away with the foot. This kick can use the whole foot. Its advantage is power. It is also useful as a block against an opponent who charges in. The instep front kick uses the instep as the striking surface. It is used to kick upward into the groin and is not legal in sparring.

Sparring Tip Since the front kick requires you to face forward, it leaves a wider target area for your opponent to score on. Practice the front kick with your body turned slightly away to reduce the target area you present. Keep both hands forward; your back arm should guard your midsection and your front arm should guard your high section.

SIDE KICK

The side kick *(yup chaki)* uses the bottom of your heel and the outer or knife edge of your foot to strike. In sparring, the side kick can strike to a middle or high target. Your target is directly in front of you, but you pivot so that your side faces the target. Then you deliver the strike.

Cock your kicking leg so that your knee is bent at least 90 degrees. Keep your foot tight by making it parallel to the floor. This is the chamber position. The higher and tighter the chamber, the more powerful the kick. Pivot on your supporting foot 180 degrees so that your toes point away from the target. Snap your kicking leg out,

extending your knee. Lean slightly over your supporting leg to maintain your balance. Strike your target with the heel of your foot. The toes of your striking foot should be either parallel to the floor or turned slightly downward. This helps you strike your target correctly. (Never strike with your toes pointing upward, as this can injure your foot and is poor technique.)

Either a front leg or back leg side kick can be used. The front leg kick is faster but the back leg kick is more powerful.

Sparring Tip   Use a front leg side kick as a feinting technique. Using quick jabs, try to get your opponent to drop his or her hands to block the kick, then follow up with a kick to the opponent's unguarded head. You can also use a chambered side kick as a block. As the opponent strikes, pull your forward leg into the side kick chamber position to block the strike. Once the opponent's strike has been blocked, strike with a side kick. This momentary delay between chamber and execution can confuse and mislead your opponent.

ROUNDHOUSE KICK

The roundhouse kick *(doll rye chaki)* strikes a target in front of you, but the kick comes from the side, moving in an arc from outside to inside. The striking surface is the instep. Lift your kicking leg from the ground and bring it in an arc from the side to the front. Your knee should be bent 90 degrees, and it should face your target. Your supporting foot should pivot 180 degrees so that your toes point away from the target. As you bring your kicking leg around, the inner side of your leg should be parallel to the ground. Sweeping forward, snap your foot out, striking the target with your instep. Your foot should be kept pointed and tight to absorb the impact of the strike.

The thrust or push roundhouse kick is done by thrusting the hips out as the kick lands, to add power. The supporting foot pivots slightly more than usual for this powerful technique.

Roundhouse kicks can also be done with the front leg or the back leg. The back leg roundhouse kick is frequently used in WTF-style fighting. Back leg kicks are also more easily countered by opponents, but this can be compensated for by practicing speed and keeping your midsection guarded.

A short roundhouse kick moves in a straight line, not an arc, to the target. Although less powerful than a traditional roundhouse kick, it is faster. It is chambered like a side kick, but the knee acts as a hinge, sweeping the foot toward the target. Advanced practitioners often use it to confuse their opponents. The opponent expects a side kick and may not be prepared to counter a roundhouse kick.

Reverse Kick

Most kicks can be done reverse. This means that instead of kicking a target directly, you turn in a half circle, then deliver the strike. You continue to rotate until you return to your original position.

In Taekwondo, the term "reverse kick" (*dwet chaki*) usually refers to the reverse side kick, sometimes called the back side kick. The kick is similar to a side kick in that your leg chambers the same way and the striking surface of the foot is the same. The difference is that your body makes a complete revolution while striking.

Stand in a back or fighting stance. The foot closest to the target is the pivot or support foot. Lift the leg farthest from the target, chambering it tightly as you would for a side kick. Bend the knee at least 90 degrees. Instead of pivoting to the front and kicking, however, spin to the back. Lean over your supporting foot to maintain your balance. Keep your kicking leg parallel to the floor. As soon as your back is to the target, turn to see the target and then strike with your foot. The heel is the striking target, and the toes should be parallel to the ground or turned down slightly. Then rechamber the kick and return to your starting position. You will have made a complete 360-degree revolution. This type of kick is extremely powerful.

Sparring Tip The reverse kick makes a good countering technique. When the opponent strikes with a roundhouse kick, for instance, immediately launch a reverse kick. This will catch the opponent in the unguarded middle section. The reverse kick is usually not a good lead-off or attacking technique since it can be anticipated by the opponent.

Intermediate Kicks

Once the basic kicks are mastered, you can add variety to your sparring by using intermediate kicking techniques. These build on the basics, so you must have a thorough understanding of the four "foundation" kicks of Taekwondo before attempting the more difficult intermediate techniques. Using a combination of basic and intermediate kicks will leave your competitors wondering what you're going to do next—which is exactly what you want!

DOUBLE KICK

One of the best ways to catch your opponent off guard is to use a double kick. What this simply means is that you strike with a kick and then, without putting your foot down, strike again. A double roundhouse kick, then, would be two roundhouse kicks in a row without putting your foot down. This tactic is especially good to use when the first kick is to the middle section (photo a, page 25) and the second kick is to the high section (photo b, page 25). The first kick to the middle draws the opponent's hands down to guard the middle section, leaving the high section unguarded, thus allowing your second kick—this one to the high section—to land unblocked. The double kick technique requires considerable speed.

Another combination is to perform a double kick that makes use of two different types of kicks. For example, you might perform a side kick to the ribs, then reach up and perform a roundhouse kick to the head. Since it is coming at a slightly different angle from the side kick, even if your partner is anticipating a double kick, he or she may not be able to block or avoid it.

Any direct kick, such as front kick, side kick, roundhouse kick, hooking kick, even reverse kick, can be made into a double kick. Circular kicks, such as crescent kicks, however, cannot be done this way.

Sparring Tip Although double kicks are usually most effective when they're done quickly—two fast kicks right in a row—smart fighters will sometimes anticipate this tactic. Instead of dropping their hands to guard their middle section, they'll keep their high section guarded. Or they'll block the first kick with a chambered side kick, keeping their high section guarded at the same time. Instead of letting a smart opponent frustrate you, practice double kicks with a pause between them. This slight delay can cause the opponent to reconsider his or her strategy. For example, the opponent might drop his or her guard. Or the opponent might launch a strike. This allows you to strike with the second kick unblocked to the target.

CRESCENT KICKS

Crescent kicks *(chiki chaki)* are circular kicks. The striking surface is either the inner or the outer edge of the foot, depending on what direction the kick is coming from. The two kinds of crescent kicks are inside-outside (uses the outer edge) and outside-inside (uses the inner edge). There is also a variation, called an axe kick, which uses the heel.

In a crescent kick, the kicking leg travels in an arc, moving across the body. The leg is swung up as high as possible, then brought down quickly.

Inside-Outside Crescent Kick

Lift your kicking leg from the ground. Sweep it forward, coming slightly across your body (photo a, page 26), and swing it as far upward as you can. Continue the kick by sweeping to the side in a circular movement (photo b, page 26). This is the actual strike. The outer edge of the foot is the striking surface and should be used to strike a high target area (shoulder or head, for instance). Finish the kick by landing with your foot in the same position it started from.

Inside-outside crescent kick.

Outside-Inside Crescent Kick

This kick is performed just like the inside-outside kick, only it travels in the opposite direction. Lift your kicking leg from the ground (photo a). Sweep to the side, bringing your leg as high up as possible. Pull your leg slightly across your body. This is the actual strike (photo b). The inner edge of the foot is the striking surface. The target area should be high. Finish by landing with your foot in the same position it started from.

Outside-inside crescent kick.

Axe Kick

The axe kick is a crescent kick modified slightly for more power. It can be performed either outside-inside or inside-outside. The only difference is the direction of the kick. In an axe kick, the striking surface is the heel of the foot. As the crescent kick reaches the top of its arc, either moving toward the body (outside-inside crescent kick) or away from the body (inside-outside crescent kick), pull your leg downward sharply and quickly, striking the top of the target with the back of your heel. Then return your foot to its starting position.

HOOKING KICK

The hooking kick *(ap hurya chaki)* strikes with the back of the heel. It is sometimes called a reverse roundhouse. The kicking foot travels past the target, then snaps back to the target, making a hooking motion. Lift your kicking leg and chamber as you would for a side kick. Instead of kicking with the bottom of your foot, however, you will be striking with the back of your heel. Therefore, as you extend your leg and straighten your knee, your foot will go past the target. Then, snap your foot to the back, through the target, with a hooking motion. The back of your heel strikes the target.

This technique is great for feinting. Your opponent will expect a side kick, but you will hook back to the target instead of striking directly at it. This makes most blocks ineffective. The hooking kick is hard for the opponent to avoid, but it must be done with speed to be effective.

Advanced Kicks

Once you're proficient with the basic and intermediate kicks and you want to increase the effectiveness of your sparring, you're ready to move up a level. Advanced kicks allow you to do this. Although these kicks are the most difficult to master, don't let that deter you from trying them, practicing them, and using them in your sparring. Incorporating advanced kicking techniques can make you virtually impossible to beat.

SPINNING WHEEL KICK

Also known as the spinning heel kick, this technique looks very difficult to do but is in fact fairly simple. The striking surface is the back of your heel. It is performed by spinning backward, pivoting on one foot with the other leg extended straight out, knee locked. The heel of the extended leg strikes the target.

Start in a strong fighting stance. As with the reverse kick, you will spin to the back to strike your target. Therefore, your forward leg is your supporting leg, and you will shift your weight to that leg. As you shift your weight to the supporting leg, extend the back leg out, keeping the knee straight (photo a). Spin on your supporting foot so that the heel of your back leg moves toward the target (photo b). Keep your heel straight by bending your ankle at a 90-degree angle. Lean over your supporting foot to maintain your balance and to add height to your kick. Spin through the target and return to the starting position.

The spinning wheel kick is a very quick technique. It can be used like the reverse kick to counter many techniques, but it is harder to block than the reverse kick. It cannot easily be used to the middle section, so consider it a high section technique only; your heel should strike head or shoulder high.

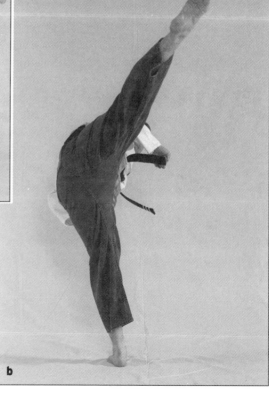

JUMP SIDE KICK

This variation of the side kick includes a jump. To perform a jump side kick *(eidan yup chaki)*, stand in a horse stance. Your feet should be about one and a half shoulder widths apart, your body and feet should face forward, and your knees should be bent as close to 90 degrees as possible. Your target is to the side, so turn your head to see the target. Move your supporting leg in so that it almost touches the foot of your kicking leg. Chamber your kicking leg by picking it up high and cocking the knee 90 degrees. Kick straight out to the side. No turning or pivoting is necessary.

As you become more proficient with the technique, you will jump as you move your supporting leg so that both feet are off the ground at the same time. Then, you will strike out with your kick, rechamber, and land. A variation of the jump side kick, sometimes called the flying jump side kick, is performed by standing several feet from your target, taking several running steps, and then performing a jump side kick. Although impressive, it is rarely, if ever, used in sparring.

Sparring Tip The jump side kick is useful in sparring when you want to close the distance to your opponent quickly. A slide or step can be used instead of the jump; such a kick is used for covering ground without losing your balance.

JUMP FRONT KICK

The jump front kick *(eidan ap chaki)* simply adds a jump to the front kick. Stand with your feet close together, facing the target. Crouch so that your knees bend about 45 degrees. The rest of your body should remain upright. Spring from the crouch, jumping into the air. As your feet leave the ground, chamber your leg and kick out with the ball of your foot.

In sparring, the jump front kick can be used to add height to the front kick, but it should be used sparingly since other techniques are faster and more powerful. A variation is sometimes used in which the martial artist jumps, feints with the left foot, but then actually kicks with the right foot (or vice versa). The feint draws the opponent's guard away from the target area.

JUMP REVERSE KICK

This technique adds a jump to the reverse kick. To begin the jump reverse kick *(eidan dwet chaki)*, stand in a strong fighting stance. Bend your knees slightly. As you jump, chamber your back leg and kick the target with your heel. Return to the starting position. This technique adds considerable power to the reverse kick and is a must-have skill for Taekwondo practitioners who compete in WTF- or Olympic-style sparring.

Sparring Tip Use the jump reverse kick to counter roundhouse kicks and reverse punches. It is very effective against opponents who charge in; a couple of jump reverse kicks will convince them to stay out of range.

JUMP ROUNDHOUSE KICK

The jump roundhouse kick *(eidan doll rye chaki)* adds a jump to the roundhouse kick. Stand with your feet together, facing the target. Crouch so that your knees bend about 45 degrees. The rest of your body should be upright and straight. As you spring from the crouch, push off with your supporting foot, pivoting slightly to position your kick correctly. Chamber your kicking leg and sweep with your kick, striking with the top of your foot.

Like the jump front kick, this technique can add height to your kick. It should be used sparingly in sparring—as a surprise move only—since there are faster and more powerful techniques. Some martial artists feint as they would for a jump front kick (drawing the opponent's block to the front), then perform the jump roundhouse kick to the unblocked side of the head.

JUMP HOOKING KICK

This technique adds a jump to the hooking kick. The jump hooking kick *(eidan hurya chaki)* is performed in a similar way to the jump side kick. With your supporting leg, step toward your kicking leg. Lift your kicking leg and perform the hooking kick. As you become more proficient, turn the step into a jump, so that you jump toward the target with both feet off the ground at the time you strike.

This technique can cover a lot of distance, closing the gap between you and your opponent during sparring. Since your opponent may be expecting a side kick, it will often catch him or her off guard.

REVERSE JUMP HOOKING KICK

The hooking kick can be made into a reverse hooking kick by adding a rotation to the back and then striking. It can also be made into a reverse jump hooking kick by adding a rotation to the jump hooking kick (photos a-b). These techniques work well to surprise an opponent during sparring. An opponent will be expecting a reverse side kick or a spinning wheel kick and will probably be unable to defend against a reverse hooking kick. However, these techniques require considerable skill and should be practiced repeatedly and mastered before they are attempted in sparring.

Kicking Fundamentals

All kicks—whether basic, intermediate, or advanced—require certain elements for complete effectiveness. For instance, you must always kick with confidence. Although your kick may not be perfect, a confident kick can make up for many mistakes. Nevertheless, it is essential to practice kicking perfectly. Spend some time doing slow practice, working on correctly chambering, pivoting, striking with the appropriate part of the foot, rechambering, and returning to the starting position. At each workout session, practice each kick at least 10 times on each leg.

Chambering and Rechambering

The main element of good kicking technique is a good chamber. Each kick has a slightly different chamber position, but all chambers should be high and tight, which means the leg should rise as far as you can make it go and the bend at the knee (if any) should be sharp and strong. Even if you are kicking to a middle target area, a high and tight chamber is necessary for good power and proper technique. A high and tight chamber will also help you to kick to high target areas even if you aren't as flexible as you'd like to be.

Nearly as important as chambering is rechambering your kick after you have successfully completed your strike. This leaves you in a position to be ready to kick again quickly if you need to. Being prepared to attack and defend quickly is basic to sparring. For each kick, you should practice the chamber, strike, and rechamber and then return to your starting position before performing the technique again. Rechambering also allows you an extra chance to work on this essential element of kicking, the chamber.

When you practice sparring, practice chambering the side kick, front kick, and roundhouse kick in exactly the same position. That way, when you spar, you can use any of the kicks once your leg is chambered. Your opponent won't know what to expect. Some of the best tournament fighters use this secret to their great advantage.

Kicking Essentials

1. Chamber.
2. Pivot (on the supporting foot).
3. Strike (with the correct striking surface).
4. Rechamber (foot shouldn't drop at end of strike).
5. Return (to your starting position).

Gaining Speed

Speed in kicking keeps you agile and ready for your next move. If your kicks are too slow, your opponent can easily see them coming and can counter or avoid them. Thus, working on speed is essential.

One way to improve speed is to add a whipping or snapping motion at the end of the kick. Instead of sweeping or pushing with your kick, try to snap it at the moment of impact. This sharp snap generates speed and power, just the way snapping a whip works. To get the necessary snap at the end of your kick, kick forward as quickly as possible and then return your leg to the chamber position faster than you kicked. This requires you to work on kicking forward and pulling your kick back instead of relying on momentum. Practicing this way builds strength as well as speed.

Challenge yourself by setting a timer (or have a partner use a stopwatch). Try to perform as many kicks as possible in an allotted period of time. Start with 10 kicks in 30 seconds and build your speed until you can do 20 and then 30 kicks in 30 seconds.

Adding Height to Kicks

The best way to add height to your kicks is to improve your flexibility. The more flexible you are, the higher you can kick. Additional leg strength also improves the height of your kicks. And, as you practice the kicks, you will learn how to create high chambers and build the muscles needed to kick higher. Therefore, over time and with practice, your kicks will naturally get higher.

High kicks can prove frustrating for fighters who aren't as flexible as they could be. Although there are exercises you can and should do to increase your flexibility, these take time to work. Meanwhile, you can add height and reach to your kicking techniques by employing these three skills:

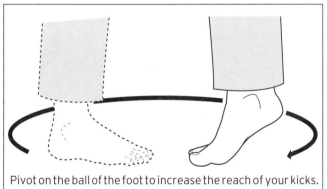
Pivot on the ball of the foot to increase the reach of your kicks.

1. Pivot on the ball of your foot. Some martial artists end up pivoting on their heels; others turn flat-footed. By learning to balance on the ball of your supporting foot, you'll be able to reach higher and farther with your kicks.

2. Lift your supporting heel off the ground as you kick. This can add several inches to your kick. (See the drawing on page 34.) For the front kick, you can go as far as to stand on your toes as you kick, since no pivot is involved. For kicks that require a pivot, you can still lift your heel off the ground and gain several inches while pivoting on the ball of your foot.

3. For kicks that require a pivot, you can add height by leaning over the supporting foot. (The photo on page 34 illustrates this leaning action.)

These quick fixes can and should be used even after you've gained additional flexibility.

Improving Jump Kicks

To improve jump kicks, you have to break the technique into its various parts. For example, a jump front kick can be broken into the jump and the front kick. Practice jumping first without worrying about the front kick. Stand with your feet together, facing the target. Crouch, bending your knees about 45 degrees, then jump as high as you can. Practice jumping until you can jump high and maintain your balance easily. Then put the jump and the kick together, going slowly at first, then faster as you become better at it.

For the jump reverse kick, try jumping and tucking your legs as tightly under you as possible. Try to make your calves touch your thighs. This helps you jump higher and puts your kicking leg in a better position to chamber and kick from. For the jump side kick and jump hooking kick, practice traveling with enough speed so that both feet are off the ground at the time that you strike. Use explosive speed and power drills to improve your ability to jump (see chapter 8).

Lift your heel off the ground to add height to your kicks and increase balance, focus, and power.

Lean over the supporting foot to make up for a lack of flexibility.

Defensive Techniques

In order to avoid your opponent's attacks, you should work on certain defensive techniques and maneuvers. These include blocks, which keep your opponent's techniques from landing on a target area, and body movements, which shift you out of the line of attack.

Blocks

Whenever you block during a sparring match, remember to keep one hand guarding your body, and in position to guard your head, at all times. Sometimes a fighter will deliberately try to force you to make a block so that you leave your body unguarded or open; then the fighter will deliver the strike that was really intended all along. For this reason, most blocks should be performed with the forward arm, with the back arm in the position to cover the body and the head if needed.

Basic Blocks

Two basic, easily learned blocks are essential for sparring. The low block protects the middle section and the high block protects the high section. These blocks should be mastered in the early stages of sparring practice in order to gain the necessary proficiency to guard against the opponent's attacks.

LOW BLOCK

The low block *(hadan maki)* is used to deflect punches and kicks delivered to the middle or low section, using the inner surface (the fleshy part) of the arm as the blocking surface. Make a fist with the hand of your blocking arm. Bring your blocking arm up to your opposite shoulder, palm facing the ceiling. With a sweeping motion, bring your arm down across your body, turning your wrist so that your palm faces toward you. Your arm should stop slightly beyond your knee or leg. Keep your wrist and hand strong in case of contact with the kick or punch that you are blocking.

The low block is useful for sweeping kicks and punches out of the way, often leaving your opponent unguarded. Take advantage of this by striking with the nonblocking hand or kicking.

Sparring Tip Since the starting or chamber position for this block is at the shoulder, the elbow rests about waist high. Learn to drop your elbow to protect your side and middle section without having to sweep down with your hand. This is a fast way to guard your middle section. Although such a block doesn't actually sweep or push the opponent's hand or foot out of the way (which is what you would want it to do in a self-defense situation, for instance), it does prevent the technique from scoring a point.

HIGH BLOCK

The high block *(sangdan maki)* protects the head and shoulders. Like the low block, it uses the inner surface of the arm. Bend the blocking arm so that the fist is under your opposite arm, near the shoulder, palm facing down. Sweep your blocking arm up in front of your body. Keep your elbow cocked at a 45-degree angle. Your blocking arm should stop slightly above the top of your head. You should be able to see under the block. The palm of your hand and the fleshy side of your arm should face the ceiling. Keep your arm strong to protect your head from a downward strike. This block is effective against crescent kicks, axe kicks, and in a slightly modified form, spinning wheel kicks.

Sparring Tip In sparring, shorten the sweep of the block by simply raising and lowering your cocked arm to prevent a technique from scoring. A short block also keeps your arm in a better position to block an attack on the body.

Intermediate and Advanced Blocks

Once the basic blocks are mastered, more specialized blocks can be learned. Because these blocks are appropriate for specific sparring situations, when to use a specific block becomes an important consideration. In practice, work on selecting blocks that work best with different strikes, then practice repeatedly so that the block becomes second nature during sparring.

CRESCENT BLOCKS

Crescent blocks *(jungdan maki)* protect the middle section of your body, including your ribs and your solar plexus. They are performed by making a sweeping motion in front of your body. A twisting motion at the end of the block helps deflect strikes. The two kinds of crescent blocks are inside-outside blocks and outside-inside blocks, which are distinguished by the direction the block travels.

Inside-Outside Crescent Block

To perform the inside-outside block, begin with your blocking arm, hand as a fist, under your opposite arm, as with a high block. Your palm faces down and your arm is parallel to the floor (photo a). Sweep your blocking arm out from your body so that it moves toward your forward leg. As it sweeps, your forearm and fist should rise so that they are perpendicular to the ground. The elbow should be bent at a 90-degree angle. Pull your opposite (nonblocking) arm back to your side, chambering your fist with the palm up. This will prepare you to punch or to execute another block. As your blocking arm crosses your forward leg, twist your forearm so that your palm faces you (photo b). This twist helps knock away the opponent's strike. Remember to keep your side facing your target and your chest facing away so that you are less vulnerable to a strike.

This block will guard against any techniques aimed at the middle section. It is very powerful and can move the opponent out of position.

Sparring Tip Practice a short version of this block—that is, one that doesn't sweep as much. This allows you to defend against techniques without leaving your arm too far out of position to strike or defend again.

Outside-Inside Crescent Block

This block is also done with the forward arm. Your nonblocking arm should guard your middle. Reach behind with your blocking arm, twisting at the waist (photo a, page 37). Cock your elbow so that your upper arm is parallel to the floor and your forearm and fist are perpendicular to it. Your palm should face forward. Your opposite arm, hand as a fist, is in front of your body. As you sweep with the blocking arm from back to front, pull your opposite arm back so that it rests chambered at your waist, palm up and ready to strike or block. Untwist or uncoil at the waist as you sweep with the blocking arm. This explosive movement adds power to your block. As your block sweeps across your forward leg, twist your wrist so that your palm faces you (photo b).

This block will guard against any technique aimed at the middle section, but it is particularly effective against strikes that come at an angle, such as the roundhouse kick.

Sparring Tip Instead of sweeping entirely across the body with the outside-inside block, learn to use your elbow as a hinge on this technique. Begin the sweep slightly behind you, then drop your fist (as you would for a low block). This protects your middle section and deflects the opponent's technique, possibly moving him or her out of position. This works very effectively against front kicks.

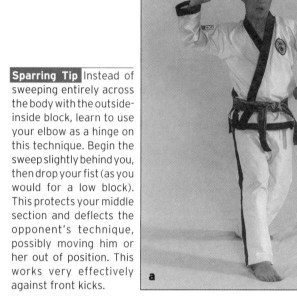

SINGLE FOREARM BLOCK

The single forearm block *(pahl maki)* protects your middle section. It is similar to a crescent block, except that it uses the inner surface of the arm as the blocking surface. Your forward arm should come up to the opposite shoulder, palm facing up. Sweep across your body with your blocking arm, keeping the elbow cocked at a 90-degree angle. As you sweep, pull the opposite arm back to chamber at your waist. As your forward arm blocks, twist your wrist so that your palm faces away from your body.

The forearm block can be used against any technique to the middle section. Although it is not as powerful as the crescent blocks, it is quicker. For this reason, it is sometimes the preferred block to use in sparring.

Nontraditional Blocks

Although they aren't necessarily taught alongside low blocks and crescent blocks, some perfectly legitimate and acceptable blocks make use of other body parts. For instance, you can draw your forward leg up into a chamber position to protect your middle section. This leaves your hands free to strike or block. It also leaves your leg in a good position to strike and can even deter an opponent from launching an attack. Some fighters use their shoulders to block attacks. They'll move their shoulder and turn their upper body slightly to ward off a technique to the upper part of the middle section. Sometimes fighters will just cover up—put a hand over their face or chest. Although they don't physically move the opponent's hand or foot out of the way, the strike is considered blocked since it lands on a nontarget area (the fighter's blocking hand). Making use of such blocks requires superior technique and plenty of experience.

Blocking Fundamentals

Blocks must be executed quickly and sharply. The momentum helps you defend against an attack. Your blocks should be as powerful as your kicks and punches.

In most cases, you will be blocking with the most muscular (fleshy) part of your arm. Most blocks have a twist at the end. It is important to perform the wrist or arm twist that is described for each block because it helps deflect the attack.

Different blocks are used to block and protect different areas. To sharpen your skills, ask a partner to strike at any section of your body, and respond with a block appropriate to that section. If you don't have a partner, call out target areas (e.g., "head" or "knee") at random and then execute an appropriate block.

Work with a partner to sharpen your blocking skills.

Other Defensive Maneuvers

As you master blocking techniques, you will learn that they have some drawbacks. Once you are committed to a block, you can't use that hand or foot to strike. If you fall for a feint, you can leave yourself open to an attack. Executing blocks takes as much energy as striking does, and yet you can't score a point blocking. For that reason, superior fighters learn alternatives to simply blocking the opponent's attacks, although blocks remain an important part of the fighter's arsenal.

Alternative defensive maneuvers in sparring include body shifting and footwork. *Body shifting*, which merely moves your body out of the way, is a simple method for avoiding attacks. *Footwork* moves you into and out of fighting range and allows you to avoid attacks without physically blocking them. This leaves you uncommitted to a block and allows you better control over the match. It also helps you set up countering techniques, which will score points.

Body Shifting

The idea of body shifting is to get your body out of the way of an attack without expending a lot of effort moving or blocking. Practice body shifting by turning your chest away from oncoming strikes.

Have a partner punch or kick directly to your middle section. Simply pivot at the waist to avoid the strikes. Have your partner add a challenge by sometimes striking at your body and sometimes striking at your head.

SHIFTING DIRECTION

Sometimes your opponent may circle around you, trying to find an opening. Instead of expending a lot of energy trying to keep up with this—and giving control of the match to your opponent—meet circling by simply shifting your fighting stance position. By changing the direction you're facing, you eliminate the circling fighter's advantage without having to circle too. As the circling opponent moves to the side or behind you, simply change the direction you face.

To change direction in a fighting stance, merely turn your upper body from front to back (photos a-b). Shift your feet so they remain perpendicular to each other in this new direction. Your front foot should point forward; your back foot should point to the side. Redistribute your weight.

By doing this, you will reserve your energy for attacking and defending. You will be able to concentrate better on your opponent if you don't allow his or her circling to get you out of your rhythm. Keep your eyes on your opponent at all times since circling is intended to distract you from what the opponent plans to do next.

Footwork

Footwork *(bal ohmkigi)* is simply the movement of your feet. As you spar, you're often unaware of where your feet are because your focus is on whether you'll be able to kick or punch in time to take advantage of an opening. However, if you are proficient with your footwork, you can move into and out of range effortlessly, and you'll be able to evade and counter your partner's techniques much more easily. It pays to spend time and effort on this.

Practice by repeating each footwork pattern several times. Then, ask a partner to punch or kick slowly while you perform a footwork pattern to evade or counter the technique. Speed up the practice as you become more competent.

FORWARD STEPPING

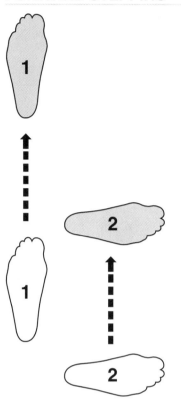

Forward stepping (also called straight stepping) is used when you are too far away to kick, or if you are in kicking range and you want to move to punching range. You simply move directly toward your target. Slide your front foot forward, then pull your back foot forward. Practice small, quick slides toward your target. To vary forward stepping—and to avoid being attacked while moving in—perform a front kick with your front leg to slide forward, then put your front leg down without rechambering and slide your back foot forward. You will be in range as soon as your kick lands.

BACKWARD STEPPING

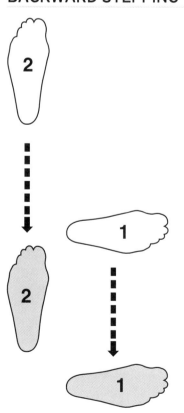

Backward stepping moves you out of the range of your opponent. It can also be used when you are in too close to use any techniques and when you are in punching range and want to move to kicking range. Slide your back foot backward, then pull your front foot backward. Practice small, quick slides away from your target. To protect yourself, you can perform a front kick with your front leg, set it down close to your back leg, then slide your back leg back into a fighting stance position.

Forward stepping and backward stepping can be combined to move you into and out of fighting range. They should be practiced together by making small, quick slides toward your target and then making small, quick slides away from your target. The faster you can move your feet, the better a fighter you'll be.

SIDE STEPPING

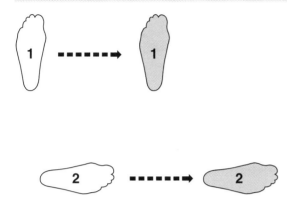

This technique is used to travel at a 90-degree angle to your opponent. It is used to move out of the way of a direct attack. A quick side step allows you to counter with your own technique. If you are stepping right, simply take a small step to the right with your left leg, away from your opponent. Your right leg should follow quickly. If you're moving to the left, do the opposite, still leading with the left foot. You must move in the direction opposite the strike in order to evade it. Practice side stepping with a variety of techniques. Often, as your opponent moves forward with a technique, you can side step it and then kick or punch to your opponent's now-exposed ribs.

PIVOT STEPPING

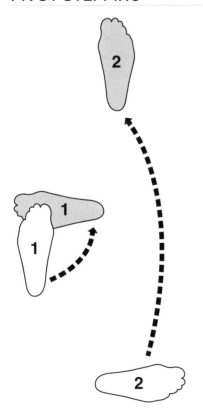

The pivot step is used to avoid any attack while you move toward or away from your opponent. To pivot step toward your opponent, push off with your rear foot and pivot in a circle on your front foot. Your opponent's attack will slide by you and you will be in a position to strike immediately. To pivot step away from your opponent, push off with your front foot and pivot in a circle on your back foot. Again, your opponent's attack will slide by you and you will be out of range of any further techniques. Pivot stepping away from an opponent can be used when your opponent is overwhelming you and you need a moment to regroup. It is better than turning your back on your opponent to avoid a strike, since this is illegal in competition and may result in a penalty.

CROSSOVER STEPPING

To cover a lot of ground while keeping your guard up, use the crossover step. Bring your back foot over your front foot so that they cross. Then slide what is now your back foot forward toward your target. Your feet will be in the same position as they were originally, except you'll be closer to your target. You can vary this technique by adding a kick to the end of it. To do this, bring your back foot over your front foot, then strike directly to the target with your back foot using a side kick or a roundhouse kick.

Proficiency in Taekwondo sparring comes from repeated training in the techniques allowed in sparring. Understanding how each technique is properly executed not only improves your sparring but also makes you a better martial artist. Each technique can be adapted slightly to be used most successfully in sparring matches. However, the techniques should also be practiced in the traditional way in order to understand how the body moves and to build the strength and flexibility needed to excel in the martial arts.

By understanding how each Taekwondo technique is executed, and knowing when to use it, you'll become a better, smarter fighter.

CHAPTER 3

TAEKWONDO TACTICS

Taekwondo is to be used not only as a means of self-defense, but also as a way of living right.

In order to become a good fighter, you'll need plenty of practice. As you try out new techniques, sequences of techniques, and defensive maneuvers, you will need a structured way to gain competence and confidence. One of the best ways to do so is through step sparring.

Step Sparring

Step sparring is a method of practicing techniques in combination to prepare for freestyle sparring. Since step sparring takes place under more controlled circumstances than freestyle sparring, it is a good way to practice. You can try out new techniques and put together different combinations of techniques to see if they work the way you expect them to. You can also improve your timing and countering skills.

Step sparring is easiest if you work with a partner, but if you don't have one, you can practice shadow sparring or you can use a heavy bag as your partner. Simply imagine that an opponent is punching or kicking, and then respond. If you do use a partner, remember to work with care. Use good control and limit contact to light touch. You should never exert full force. When you become more confident in your skills, you and your partner may agree to heavier contact, but special care should always be taken to avoid injury. If you want to step spar more realistically, consider wearing your sparring equipment.

The Attack

Have your partner launch an attack with a single technique. If you are a beginner, start by having your partner punch to your chest. As you grow more proficient, vary the routine by having your partner attack with a variety of kicks to a variety of target areas.

The Block

In the beginner and early intermediate stages of sparring, you will want to respond to your partner's strike with a block. Begin with low blocks and high blocks, incorporating other blocks as you become more comfortable with step sparring. As you become more advanced, you will quit relying on blocks to stop an attack and will use footwork and body shifting instead.

The Evasion

Blocking takes time and commits you to a technique that can't score. In the later intermediate and advanced levels of sparring, you will rely less on blocking and more on evading an opponent's attacks. As you work on step sparring, use body shifting and footwork techniques to avoid your opponent's attacks before launching your own attacks or countering techniques.

The Counter

Once you've blocked or evaded your partner's strike, you'll counter with two or three techniques that flow smoothly. Since you'll be starting from farther away and moving in, begin with kicking techniques and then move to hand techniques. Your partner should stay in place. (Having both partners moving back and forth is done in freestyle sparring, not step sparring.)

When you have finished your series of techniques, *kihop* loudly to signal that you've finished. Be sure to take turns attacking and defending so that each partner gains valuable experience.

Step Sparring Drills

The following step sparring drills will get you started. Go through them several times until you feel comfortable with each sequence, then add your own variations. Once you think you're ready to strike out on your own, feel free to make up your own step sparring sequences.

Develop a set of step sparring sequences that cover different kinds of punches and kicks. The sequences you develop should suit your style, skills, and abilities. But instead of repeating the same step sparring sequences over and over, think up several new ones at every workout session. To do this, simply respond to your partner's attacks with a fresh series of techniques each time, trying to react to your partner's kicks or punches without thinking about it. This helps you learn to respond more quickly during actual sparring matches.

To make the step sparring scenario more realistic, have both partners signal that they are ready by giving a loud *kihop*. Once the signal is given, the attacker can wait for whatever length of time he or she wishes before attacking. When the attacker varies the length of time between the ready signal and the attack, the defending partner is forced to wait for the attack to be launched before responding to it. Otherwise, he or she may be responding to the *kihop* instead of to the strike. A good fighter responds to an attack, not to a *kihop*. This variation also builds valuable timing skills.

For the following drills, the attacking partner should begin in a front stance. The chest and feet face the same direction. The feet are placed about one and a half shoulder widths apart. The forward leg is bent at the knee at a 90-degree angle. The back leg is extended straight behind, knee straight. The back foot should be flat on the floor. For step sparring, start with the left leg forward. The attacking partner should perform a low block over the left leg, then *kihop* to show readiness. The defending partner should stand naturally in a ready stance. After hearing the attacking partner's *kihop*, the defending partner should also *kihop* to signal readiness. Then, the attacking partner should step forward with the right leg, at the same time performing a straight punch with the right hand. The straight punch should be aimed at the defender's chest.

Once the following drills have been learned and are understood, change the attacking sequence. Use different stances and kicking techniques, and use both arms and legs.

COUNTER WITH PUNCHES

As your partner punches to your chest, side step to the right, away from the punch. Block the punch away with your left hand. Punch to the ribs with your right hand (photo a), then with your left (photo b). *Kihop* to signal the end of the sequence.

As a variation, add a kick to the midsection once you have the punching sequence down, as in photo c.

COUNTER WITH SIDE KICK

As your partner punches toward your chest, side step to the right away from your partner's punch. Block the punch (photo a). Perform a side kick with your right leg, striking to your partner's ribs (photo b). *Kihop* to signal the end of the sequence.

You can create a variation by adding a reverse kick. After striking with the side kick, set your kicking foot down, turn, and execute a reverse kick with your left foot, striking to your partner's ribs (photo c).

COUNTER WITH CRESCENT KICK AND HOOKING KICK

As your partner punches toward your chest, step slightly back with your left leg. Bring your left leg up in an inside-outside crescent kick, knocking your partner's punching hand away (photo a). As you land on your left foot, bring your right foot up and perform a hooking kick to the side of your partner's face (photo b). *Kihop* to signal the end of the sequence. To create a variation, add a roundhouse kick to the sequence. After striking with the hooking kick, rechamber your leg without setting it down and perform a roundhouse kick to your partner's head, as shown in photo c.

Freestyle Sparring Practice

Step sparring is a great way to introduce new techniques, counters, and defensive maneuvers into your sparring. However, you also have to practice freestyle sparring itself to become a proficient fighter. When you practice freestyle sparring, it is a good idea to keep tournament rules in mind. Although you should forget the rules every now and then and spar using every Taekwondo technique you know, for the most part you should train for tournament rules. This means using techniques, strategies, and tactics that will succeed in tournament. Dust off those nontournament techniques—such as a backfist to the head—every now and then for fun and skills enhancement.

If you don't always have a partner to spar, you can still work on techniques such as body shifting or footwork. You can also invest in a heavy bag. Durable freestanding heavy bags, which you fill with water, make a good alternative to hanging a traditional heavy bag from a ceiling joist. Sparring a heavy bag is an excellent workout and offers the opportunity to work on offensive techniques.

Shadow sparring is also an effective way to practice offensive techniques. Spar in front of a full-length mirror for the best effect. You can learn how to do techniques better and more accurately this way.

Of course, nothing is as effective as good sparring partners to improve your sparring skills. Even if you are better than some of your sparring partners, remember that you can take away insights and strategies from every martial artist you work with.

Maintaining Fighting Range

Fighting range is the most important concept a fighter can learn. The distance between you and your partner dictates the type of techniques you can perform. Fighting range is different for every person because each person has different arm and leg lengths and different reaches. Basically, if you are several feet from your partner, you are in kicking range and kicking techniques will be most effective. If you are within a foot or two of your partner, you are in punching range and punching techniques will be most effective. If you are too far from your partner for a kick to be effective, you are out of range and need to close the gap.

At the beginner level, fighters often spar very far away from each other in order to avoid contact and because they don't have confidence in their control. As you gain confidence, you should close the gap.

Sometimes fighters get too close to each other, and then no techniques are effective. When this happens, back step—using a kick to guard—to move back into fighting range. Moving into and out of the different fighting ranges requires footwork, which was discussed in chapter 2 (see pages 39 to 42).

Fighting ranges: *(a)* kicking range, *(b)* punching range, *(c)* out of range.

Assessing Your Strengths

In order to improve your sparring, you need to assess your strengths honestly. First, consider your inherent physical abilities (not your Taekwondo skills, which can improve quickly with practice). Are you quick? Agile? Powerful? Flexible? Pick techniques that match your physical abilities. Quick fighters should use front kicks, side kicks, crescent kicks, and spinning wheel kicks against opponents. If you're a quick fighter, use front leg kicks instead of back leg kicks. Practice double kicks, which will add variety to your sparring.

If you are an agile fighter, you should consider focusing on body shifting and footwork techniques to set up counters. Any type of evasive movement will help you set up your opponents. Work on moving quickly into or out of fighting range, staying light on your feet. Agile fighters can often use jumping techniques to excellent effect.

If you are a powerful fighter you should use direct, forcible techniques, such as punches, side kicks, and reverse kicks. Powerful fighters tend to be slower than other types of fighters, so you should focus on creating openings by setting up your opponent. Then you can anticipate the opening and strike powerfully.

Flexible fighters can take advantage of high kicks. Think of roundhouse kicks and hooking kicks to the head. Flexible fighters can also use double kicks, especially middle-high combinations.

Assessing Your Strengths—Physical Abilities

Quick fighters: Use front kicks, side kicks, crescent kicks, and spinning wheel kicks. Use front leg kicks instead of back leg kicks. Double kicks will add variety.

Agile fighters: Use body shifting and footwork techniques to set up counters. Move quickly into or out of fighting range. Use jumping techniques.

Powerful fighters: Use direct, forcible techniques, such as punches, side kicks, and reverse kicks. Create openings by setting up opponent.

Flexible fighters: Use high kicks, especially roundhouse kicks and hooking kicks to the head. Use double kicks, especially middle-high combinations.

Next, consider your body type. Are you tall or short or average? Are you big, small, in-between? How you answer will help you devise suitable sparring strategies. For example, if you are short but big, you can deliver power blows, but your opponents will have a longer reach. Therefore, you will need to work on techniques for getting into your fighting range without getting nailed. Use footwork techniques to get inside. Use a front kick to guard yourself while getting into range, then use powerful punches to score points. Use a solid reverse kick to get out of range again and to set up your next attack.

If you are short but small, you will use some of the same ideas. Work on getting into your fighting range without getting nailed. Use footwork for this and practice body shifting to avoid attacks. If you're small, use quick, easy scoring techniques such as front kicks and roundhouse kicks once you are in range.

Tall, big people have some advantages. They have excellent reach and powerful techniques, but they tend to be slower than people of other body types. If this is your body type, practice keeping opponents at a distance. Stop people who want to come inside by using a side kick to the ribs. Follow with a power technique such as a reverse kick. If your opponent does get inside, use powerful punches to score and to convince him or her to get out of the range of your hands.

If you are tall and light, you have the advantage of reach and quickness. With your height, you have an easier time scoring with kicks to the head. However, you must also work to keep people from coming inside. Use roundhouse kicks, especially double kicks, on opponents who try to move inside. Use footwork to keep people from moving in, since it's hard for you to fight at a small person's punching range. Master techniques for moving into your kicking range, such as back stepping and pivot stepping. You can also use jump kicks away from your target to establish a better kicking range.

If you're an average-sized person, you have to be adaptable, since your opponents won't always be either shorter or taller than you. Work on inside fighting techniques for sparring taller people and work on evasive techniques for avoiding extremely quick or powerful fighters. Remember that many of the greatest Taekwondo practitioners are average-sized people. Forced to become versatile, they turn into excellent fighters.

Assessing Your Strengths—Body Type

Short and big: Use power blows. Footwork techniques will allow you to get inside. Use a front kick to guard while getting into range, then use powerful punches to score points. A solid reverse kick will help you get out of range again and set up your next attack.

Short and small: Use footwork to get inside, and practice body shifting to avoid attacks. Use quick, easy scoring techniques such as front kicks and roundhouse kicks once you are in range.

Tall and big: Keep opponents at a distance. Stop people with a side kick to the ribs. Follow with a power technique (e.g., reverse kick).

Tall and light: Use high kicks. Keep opponents from coming inside. Use double kicks to stop opponents. Footwork such as back stepping and pivot stepping will help move you into kicking range.

Average-sized: Be adaptable. Work on inside fighting techniques for sparring taller people and evasive techniques for avoiding extremely quick or powerful fighters.

Although making an honest assessment of yourself is essential to finding a style of fighting that works best for you, don't limit yourself. Don't turn into a one-dimensional fighter. Even if you are small and light, you can improve your strength and power. If you are big and powerful, you can work on your flexibility and speed. In order to spar to the best of your ability, you should condition yourself. Flexibility training, speed training, and power training are all important elements to your success as a fighter. See chapter 8 for drills to improve your flexibility, speed, and power.

Success in sparring, as in Taekwondo itself, is not a finite goal, but a matter of being willing to embark on an ongoing process.

PART II

KARATE SPARRING

CHAPTER 4
KARATE ESSENTIALS

The concern of the martial artist is not only to master techniques, but to learn one's capacity for spontaneous expression in the natural order and rhythm of life.

If you are looking to improve your sparring skills, you may already be enrolled in a class at a formal martial arts school. If this is the case, remember that your instructor is your primary teacher. If your instructor does not allow knee strikes at all during practice sparring, for example, show respect and don't use them. If your instructor has suggestions for improving your sparring, take heed. Take what you can from the information available, whether it is from this book, from your instructor, or from other martial artists. By applying the principles that work for you, you will become a better martial artist.

This chapter covers the basic information you need to select workout clothing and gear. It also provides a detailed description of sparring in competition, including the rules of the main sanctioning organization.

Clothing and Equipment

Choosing the right workout clothing and the right protective equipment will make your sparring practice go more smoothly and will help prevent injury. The following guidelines will help you make appropriate choices.

Workout Clothes

Although there are dozens of Karate styles, each with its own rules and practices, Karate practitioners tend to be less formal and less traditional than Taekwondo practitioners. For this reason, they may not wear uniforms when practicing, preferring loose-fitting sweatpants and a T-shirt. However, some Karate practitioners feel that taking off their street clothes and putting on the uniform reminds them of their connection and obligations to the martial arts. Just as putting on a business suit can make one feel ready for business, putting on a Karate uniform can make one feel ready for Karate.

In either case, it's important to dress appropriately for a workout. Use these guidelines as you make your choices.

1. Clothing should not be restrictive. You should be able to move freely so that your kicks and punches flow naturally. At the same time, your workout clothing shouldn't be so loose that it catches on your opponent's arms and legs. This can cause damage to both of you!

2. If you choose to wear a sweatsuit or shorts and a T-shirt, be certain to keep your shirt tucked in. Some Karate practitioners wear their rank belt even while practicing in casual workout clothing in order to keep their shirt from coming untucked.

3. If you decide to wear a traditional uniform, make certain the top stays closed at all times. Since the traditional Karate *gi* closes like a bathrobe, this can be a problem occasionally. A gaping uniform top can catch an opponent's hand or foot and can be dangerous. Use a safety pin to prevent the top from coming open. Some martial artists also report success using Velcro to keep their tops closed.

4. Never wear makeup or jewelry while sparring. When you sweat, makeup runs. It stings when it gets in your eyes and can stain clothing. Jewelry can be dangerous. It can scratch your partner and can catch in your (or your partner's) clothing. Remember to remove necklaces, rings, and earrings before working out. Replace regular glasses with contact lenses or safety glasses especially designed for sports.

Protective Gear

Because many Karate practitioners believe the use of safety equipment encourages excessive contact, the use of too much equipment is discouraged. Most Karate styles emphasize control and technique in sparring rather than hitting as hard as possible.

That said, protective gear is sometimes used, especially in practice sessions. Sparring gear (also called sparring equipment) consists simply of padded protectors that keep you and your partner from getting bruised, especially if you accidentally kick too hard or if you happen to block an elbow instead of an arm. If you are working on new techniques and want to try them in sparring, it can be a good idea to wear sparring equipment so that you don't accidentally hurt your partner when you lose control of your takedown technique. The pros and cons of some of the most common pieces of sparring equipment are discussed here.

Headgear

Many Karate practitioners think headgear actually contributes to injuries by encouraging heavier contact and lack of control. Therefore, headgear is not worn in most Karate competitions. However, headgear, like a helmet, can protect the sides and back of your head from kicks and punches. Headgear can be purchased with a masklike face protector so that a strike to the face doesn't break the nose.

Mouthguard

The mouthguard is an essential item and is almost always required in competition. The mouthguard protects the teeth from jarring blows that can cause cracks and other dental problems. Mouthguards are sold in several sizes for adults and children and can be custom fitted easily.

Chest Protector

Very few Karate practitioners use chest protectors. Some female competitors choose to wear them and in some tournaments this is allowed. If you spar with fairly heavy contact, a chest protector can be a wise investment. Most Karate practitioners, however, find them cumbersome and feel they inhibit techniques. Unless you have an injury such as a cracked rib, you should probably skip the chest protector.

Groin Protector

If you're a man, you need one of these. No sparring in tournaments is allowed without one, and as anyone who has tried will tell you, you don't want to practice sparring without one. Groin protectors are also available for women, but they are usually considered unnecessary and even dangerous.

Forearm Guards

Forearm guards protect the forearms from bumps and bruises that occur when blocking kicks and punches. They are usually not allowed in Karate tournament competitions.

Hand Protectors

Hand protectors protect your partner in case your hand technique lands too hard or inaccurately. They come in several varieties and are made of either padded cotton or plastic-covered foam. The most common type covers the back of the hand with a strap that wraps around the wrist. Another type, usually made of leather, is the glove-style hand protector, which looks like a fingerless glove with some padding on the back. This type is excellent to use for open hand techniques because it doesn't restrict the movement of the hand. However, it may not be accepted at tournaments, so be sure to have a pair of backup protectors. Hand protection of some sort is usually required in Karate competition.

Shin Guards

Shin guards, designed to protect the shins from bumps and bruises, can be useful for practicing sparring, especially if you use your legs to block strikes. They are banned in international Karate competition and may be banned in other competitions as well.

Foot Protectors

Foot protectors protect your partner against a kick that lands too hard or inaccurately. They are often banned in Karate competition since they are believed to encourage harder kicking. For practice sparring, they can be very useful.

There are three main types of foot protectors. One type slides onto the foot, protecting the top or instep of the foot. It wraps around the ankle to stay in place. Another type is a combination foot protector/shin guard. It is all one piece and covers both the shin and the instep with a layer of padding. Neither of these protectors cover the heel or the bottom of the foot. The third type of foot protector covers the entire foot, including the toes and the sides of the feet. It attaches with a strap that goes around the foot. This type is preferred by martial artists who perform kicks that use the heel as the striking surface. Its only drawback is that it is a little heavier and more cumbersome than the other types.

Hand protectors

Karate sparring equipment.

Where to Find Uniforms and Equipment

To enter formal competition, you will need to be outfitted with the appropriate uniform and gear. Make certain that any uniform you purchase is specifically a Karate *gi*.

If you are taking formal lessons from an instructor, he or she can often provide uniforms and sparring gear at a reasonable cost. If not, many larger sporting goods stores carry various lines of martial arts equipment. Some larger cities have martial arts supply stores. You can also purchase martial arts equipment through the following mail-order houses, which will send catalogs at your request:

American Martial Arts Supply
5848 East Speedway Boulevard
Tucson, AZ 85712
Telephone: 800-283-1299
520-740-0479
www.amas.net

Century Martial Arts Supply, Inc.
1705 National Boulevard
Midwest City, OK 73110
Telephone: 800-626-2787
405-732-2226
www.centuryma.com

Macho Products, Inc.
10045 102nd Terrace
Sebastian, FL 32958
Telephone: 800-327-6812
561-388-9892
www.macho.com

Pil Sung Martial Art Supply, LLC.
6300 Ridglea Place, Suite 1008
Fort Worth, TX 76116
Telephone: 800-992-0388
817-738-5408
www.pil-sung.com

Practice Matches

Because you and your partner decide the rules for practice sparring matches, they can have as many or as few rules as you agree on. Sometimes Karate fighters will agree that kicks to the knee or groin strikes are acceptable in order to mimic street fighting. This makes the match more realistic.

For the most part, however, practice sparring follows set rules. The legal target areas usually include

- the chest (including the sides),
- the back,
- the neck,
- the sides of the head, and
- the face.

In other words, everything above the pubic bone is a legal target area, with the following exceptions. Illegal target areas include

- the throat,
- the back of the head,
- the legs, and
- the groin.

In practice sparring, all kicking techniques are legal to all target areas. Knee strikes are often allowed. Closed and open hand techniques are usually legal to all target areas. Takedowns, throws, and sweeps are frequently allowed.

The amount of contact allowed can vary, depending on the partners. No contact or light contact is usually the rule for beginners, light-to-medium contact for intermediate practitioners, and medium-to-heavy contact for advanced fighters. Most sparring is done semicontact; only professional Karate practitioners spar full contact.

After agreeing with your partner about how much contact is acceptable, use good control to stay within those bounds. Also, be sure to respect your partner's wishes if he or she asks you to lessen your intensity level. While it is unrealistic to think you won't acquire some bruises during a sparring match, a good martial artist doesn't need to pound on his or her partner to prove fighting prowess. A truly talented martial artist can score points and make contact with a partner without leaving bruises behind. Excellent control is the hallmark of the superior martial artist.

As in Taekwondo sparring, Karate sparring is usually held in continuous rounds (no stopping) for one or two minutes at a time. The length of practice sessions is determined by the partners. While partners usually do not keep formal score of points, they may use an informal acknowledgment system in which each partner acknowledges when a legal technique has landed, unblocked, to a legal target area. This is usually done by tapping the area that was struck or by saying, "point."

Competition

Karate freestyle sparring competition is called *kumite*. Attacks are judged according to accuracy, power, and effectiveness, although competitors are expected to exercise excellent control. The competitors are also judged on mental, personal, and physical development. The fighter who exercises good control; who appears focused; who arrives wearing a clean uniform; and who treats opponents, judges, and others with courtesy is considered a well-developed fighter. Good technique and an impressive physique are only part of the equation.

Fighters are expected to wear clean, white *karate-gi* (uniforms). An approved *gi* has sleeves that cover at least half of the forearms but not the wrists. The jacket must cover the hips but shouldn't extend past mid-thigh. Women are allowed to wear a white T-shirt beneath the jacket. The pants cover at least two thirds of the shin, but cannot touch the floor. Pant legs and sleeves are never rolled up.

A few pieces of safety equipment are required for international competition: hand protectors, mouthguards, and for men, groin protectors. Women are sometimes allowed to use chest protectors. In other tournaments, other safety equipment, such as headgear, shin guards, and the like, may be acceptable.

WKF-Sanctioned Tournaments

Although there are literally dozens of Karate styles with their own rules and sponsoring organizations, many competitions are held following World Karate Federation (WKF) rules. WKF tournaments are the most common types, and most other organizations base their tournament rules on WKF rules. However, it pays to check the tournament rules sheets and to ask questions of the tournament organizers so that you can be sure to practice in an appropriate way.

Tournament Divisions

Karate *kumite* competition is held between individuals and between teams. Competitors are assigned to divisions based on age, rank, gender, and weight. Depending on the number of competitors, divisions can be broad (red belt men) or narrow (first degree black belt men, adult [ages 18 to 35] lightweight division).

Length of Matches

A Karate sparring match usually consists of one round of two to three minutes. Under WKF rules, the first person to reach three points wins. If neither competitor reaches three points before the end of the match, the person who is ahead wins the match. If both competitors are tied at the end of the match, the referee asks for a decision. The referee and judges decide whether to award the match to one of the competitors, such as the one with superior technique or a better attitude, or whether to announce a draw. If the referee and judges agree that the match ended in a draw, a sudden-death match then takes place. In this case, the first competitor to score a point wins the match. If the match is still tied at the end of the sudden-death period, the referee again calls for a decision and the referee and judges must award the win to one of the competitors.

Ring Size

The ring is 8 meters by 8 meters (about 26 feet by 26 feet). The boundary line is considered in bounds. A warning zone, which is 1 meter (about 3.3 feet) inside the ring, reminds competitors they are nearing the out-of-bounds area.

Judges

Under WKF rules, a referee, one or more judges, and an arbitrator judge sparring competitions. The most common judging system, especially in international competition, is the two-flag system. In this type of competition, the referee watches the competitors, moves about the ring, judges the match, awards points and fouls, and decides the outcome of the match. The judges assist by indicating scores with their flags. This information is used by the referee to decide the match, but the judges themselves do not award points. The arbitrator ensures that the rules are followed and that the match is conducted according to the stated guidelines, but he or she does not have a say in the outcome of the match. The arbitrator also serves as timekeeper and scorekeeper.

Head and face

Neck (excluding throat)

Back

Chest and abdomen

Legal target areas in Karate sparring.

Legal Target Areas

The head, face, and neck are all legal target areas and are considered the "high" section. The chest, abdomen, and back are also legal target areas and are considered the "middle" section. The shoulder blades are considered part of the back, but the shoulders themselves are not a legal target area. The abdomen includes the area below the belt to the pubic bone. The throat itself is not a legal target area.

Point Criteria

Competitors attempt to score points on one another through the use of acceptable Karate techniques. These points are called *ippon* and *waza-ari,* and are often compared to "point" and "half-point" or "almost point."

Certain criteria must be present for a point *(ippon)* to be awarded. If a technique is not quite an *ippon,* a *waza-ari* may be awarded. Two *waza-ari* scores can be combined to equal one point. If any criterion is completely missing, no score is allowed.

Six Criteria to Score *Ippon* (One Point)

- *Correct form.* The technique must be executed properly.
- *Correct attitude.* The fighter must deliberately intend to score. A *kiai* or shout delivered at the time of the strike helps to show correct attitude.
- *Powerful application.* The fighter must deliver the technique with confidence and power.
- *Correct distance.* The fighter must be neither too close nor too far away from the opponent when delivering a strike. An appropriate amount of contact should be used.
- *Correct timing.* The fighter must be able to deliver a blow that if completely extended and performed at full power could cause damage to the opponent. This means that partly blocked strikes or those coming from the wrong angle do not score.
- *Mental alertness (zanshin).* The fighter must maintain a state of continued awareness and focus after the blow has been delivered; this is often called a warrior mind-set.

Some techniques are scored as *ippon* even if they are of *waza-ari* quality. These include high kicks (to the head or face); scoring at the moment the opponent attacks; blocking an attack and countering to the unguarded target area; sweeps or throws followed by a scoring technique; and delivering more than one strike in a row, with all strikes landing and the opponent unable to interrupt or stop the flow. These techniques earn either a full *ippon* or no score at all.

Scoring Points

Karate tournament sparring competitions are not fought continuously. The sparring is stopped for several different reasons, such as when a point is scored or a penalty assessed.

Reasons for Stoppage of Play

- A technique scores.
- A penalty occurs.
- Either competitor breaks a rule.
- A competitor is injured or shows other signs of distress.
- A competitor grabs the opponent without following up with a takedown or other acceptable technique.
- Either or both competitors fall to the ground with no follow-up techniques.
- There is confusion or misunderstanding during the match.

If the referee sees a score, he announces which fighter has scored, the type of technique used (punch, kick) and whether the score is *ippon* or *waza-ari*. A score cannot occur after time is called or if there is a pause in play, for instance because one fighter has stepped out of bounds. A competitor who is out of bounds cannot score on one who is in bounds. A competitor who is in bounds can score on an opponent who is out of bounds if he or she does so before the referee calls for a stoppage of play. This helps prevent competitors from stepping out of bounds to avoid a score.

If both fighters deliver a scoring technique simultaneously, neither is awarded a score. Competitors are allowed to grab each other, but a scoring technique must follow immediately. Fighters may also fight from the floor, but the referee will usually stop play to prevent injury.

Rules Infractions

Warnings or fouls are called if either competitor does not obey the rules. If a competitor breaks the rules, the referee might award a point to the opponent or might give the opponent the win. The referee can choose to give an unofficial warning, a *waza-ari* penalty, an *ippon* penalty, a loss of match penalty, or a disqualification.

Penalties for Rules Infractions

- Unofficial warning (the referee reminds the fighter to obey the rules but no point is added to the opponent's score).
- *Waza-ari* penalty (in which *waza-ari* is added to the opponent's score)
- *Ippon* penalty (in which *ippon* is added to the opponent's score)
- Loss of match penalty.

- Disqualification (Disqualification can occur when a competitor has a serious disregard for the rules of competition. Disqualification can be imposed without other warnings or penalties. Competitors can be suspended or banned from competition for life.)

Fouls such as stepping out of bounds usually receive a warning first and then escalate through the sequence of penalties. If a fighter lacks control, however, he or she can be penalized right away; the referee need not give a warning first. The referee makes the decision based on the fighter's intent (accidents are treated less seriously than intentional infractions) and the degree of any injury that occurs. Once a fighter receives a warning or penalty, the penalty must escalate for the same infraction. For example, a fighter may earn a *waza-ari* penalty because a technique lacked control and he injured an opponent. If he is called for the same foul again (lack of control), he must be penalized *ippon,* even if this time his lack of control is less serious.

Infractions Resulting in Warnings or Penalties

- Stepping out of bounds
- Failing to follow the referee's instructions
- Circling and other movements that waste time (Fighters must attack/counterattack quickly.)
- Repeated retreating to avoid the opponent
- Exaggerating or faking an injury
- Lack of regard for personal safety
- Attempting to score after play has been stopped for any reason
- Attacking the groin, joints, or instep
- Attacking to the face with open hand techniques
- Contact of any kind to the throat area
- Dangerous throws
- Techniques that by nature are not controllable, including blind techniques
- Repeatedly attacking arms or legs
- Lack of control to any target area

Acts Resulting in Disqualification

- Behavior that harms Karate (discourtesy, swearing, and poor sportsmanship)
- Disobeying the referee
- Acting in a dangerous manner
- Becoming overexcited/aggressive and interfering with the flow of the match
- Faking an injury
- Deliberately violating the rules of the tournament
- If injured, returning to the contest or match area without the consent of the physician

Other Types of Competition

There are many styles of Karate and many organizations that sponsor competitions. For this reason, the rules of any specific tournament will vary. For instance, at some local and regional tournaments, kicks to the head are illegal in sparring competition and can result in a warning, an assessed penalty, or even a disqualification. Therefore, it is important to know the contest rules ahead of time.

In traditional Japanese systems, the one-point system is sometimes used. In this case, the first fighter to score a full point *(ippon)* wins the match. Thus, competitors must be aggressive in order to score first, but must have excellent defense in order not to lose the match on the first strike. In some Karate tournaments, if a match is tied, competitors break boards to determine the winner.

A "Grand Champion" match is frequently held at Karate tournaments. Black belt fighters who have won their division spar each other to determine the single best contestant. These usually require two bouts of two minutes each with a minute rest between.

In semicontact Karate, more protective gear is worn and medium contact is allowed. Various rules are employed, but usually two-minute matches are used with the accumulated point system. Excessive contact results in penalties and possible disqualification.

Professional Karate, also known as full contact, is fought to the knockout. In this case, for a technique to score it must land with visible contact and it must be unblocked.

By using and wearing appropriate equipment and workout clothing, the Karate fighter can prevent many injuries and can practice sparring in a comfortable way. By understanding the rules of Karate sparring competition, the fighter can practice in an appropriate way. Even if you don't plan to compete, learning and understanding the rules improves your sparring and makes certain that all sparring partners are following the same guidelines.

CHAPTER 5

KARATE TECHNIQUES

The truth is, skills are secondary to the right motivation.

Karate practitioners learn many different techniques. By understanding which ones are used in competition, the martial artist can practice most effectively. Since some Karate techniques don't score points in competition, you will want to practice those techniques that are most likely to score. For example, spinning wheel kicks don't meet the criterion of controlled power, so it is hard to score points using them. Many judges will simply disregard wheel kicks. Therefore, you would be better off practicing techniques that will score, such as front kicks and elbow strikes.

Legal Techniques

Although Karate practitioners have many different techniques at their disposal, not all of these are allowed in sparring. For example, although a two-finger strike to the face could stop an attacker, it's not allowed in competitive sparring. Although you may practice with whatever techniques you and your partners mutually agree on, if you plan to spar in tournament competition, you would do well to practice using only "legal techniques"— those allowed in competition.

Many but not all competitions allow fighters to use open hand techniques to any target area. Be certain the competition you are preparing for allows such techniques. If not—or if you are unsure—it is best to practice as if they were not allowed.

Although some competitions limit the types of Karate techniques used in sparring matches, most allow any Karate technique with the exception of finger strikes to the eyes and strikes using the head. In addition, strikes to the groin, legs, and throat are not legal.

Stances

Karate fighters use a few different stances in competition. Although most techniques are performed in the fighting stance, other stances should be practiced. That way you won't be considered discourteous, for instance, for failing to stand in an attention stance at the appropriate time.

ATTENTION STANCE

At the beginning of a competition, fighters usually bow to each other and the referee and judges (if any). To do so, they assume the attention stance, in which the heels are placed together and the toes are turned out. The arms are placed against the sides. The fighter focuses straight ahead.

OPEN LEG STANCE

Once the courtesies are completed, the fighters assume a natural, open leg stance in which the feet are placed about shoulder-width apart and the hands are held as fists in front of the hips, elbows slightly bent.

FIGHTING STANCE

When fighters are asked to assume the fighting stance, they might choose from among several possibilities. In the *back stance*, one foot points straight ahead, the other at a 90-degree angle to it. The back leg bears more weight than the front leg. Both knees are bent slightly outward. The body, including the chest, is turned to the side to provide a smaller target area.

The *cat stance* is used for quick attacks and blocks and for moving quickly from one position to another. Weight is supported on the back leg, which is turned about 45 degrees to the side. Knees and ankles are slightly bent. The hips may face front or side; the chest faces front in order to strike directly at the opponent.

A *modified back stance* is often used for sparring. In this case, the chest is turned more toward the opponent and the legs assume a more natural position, although one remains behind the other. Fighting stances are usually low and solid.

In most fighting stances, the hands start in the middle guard position. The forward arm is bent at the elbow and is held a few inches away from the body. The elbow should be tucked to protect the ribs. The fist covers the chest. The back hand is held tightly chambered. The chamber is the "ready" position of the striking arm; this ready position is different for different techniques. In this case, it means the elbow is bent at a 90-degree angle, and the arm is held in front of the solar plexus, with the hand held slightly above the elbow.

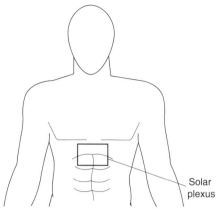

Start the *kiai* by summoning your breath from the solar plexus.

Solar plexus

Kiai or Shout

In sparring matches, Karate competitors summon their energy and focus their concentration by using the *kiai* or shout. Whenever you launch an attack with the intention of scoring a point, a loud *kiai* helps you to focus on your purpose. It also draws the judges' attention so that they are more likely to notice when you score a point. A *kiai* can show that you had the correct intention to score, which is one of the criteria for achieving *ippon*. For these reasons, it is important to develop a good *kiai*.

Begin by taking a deep breath. As you exhale slowly, find your solar plexus (located between your sternum and your navel) and push in. This should forcibly expel your breath. Now that you have an idea of where the energy comes from, remember your solar plexus as you summon your breath to *kiai*. Using only your lungs will result in a weaker, higher-pitched yell. Also, remember that a scream is not a shout. Young people in particular often make this mistake. Your *kiai* should start deep in your body and focus all of your attention and energy. Good *kiai* during a sparring match can help you win the match.

Hand Techniques

In Karate, many closed hand techniques are used, the variations being the striking surface used. Both open and closed hand techniques are allowed in most sparring matches. The Karate fighter must master a complete arsenal of hand techniques or risk being at a serious disadvantage.

Basic Hand Techniques

Karate is known for its wide variety of hand techniques. But even the basic punching techniques can be used to excellent effect in Karate sparring. Some practitioners use punches 80 percent of the time or more when they use hand techniques. Therefore, it is important to practice and master these "foundation" techniques.

FOREFIST

The forefist *(seiken)* starts with a strong fist. Roll your fingers into a tight ball, then "lock" them in place by closing your thumb across the index and middle finger. The striking surface is the foreknuckles of your index and middle finger. The wrist should be straight and the hand and arm should be in a line.

STRAIGHT PUNCH

The straight punch *(choku-tsuki)* is a fast punch using the front hand, like a jab in boxing. Make a fist by rolling your fingers into a ball and folding your thumb over. The hand should be tight. The first two knuckles of your fist make up the striking area. Your wrist and hand should remain in a straight line. Chamber your arm at your side by pulling your arm back and bending your elbow at a 90-degree angle. Your palm should be facing up. Punch forward with your arm. At the end of the strike, twist your wrist so that your palm faces down. This is done to add explosive power to the impact of your punch.

The punch usually extends from slightly above the waist forward, with the power of your shoulder and hips behind it. But to use this technique in sparring, chamber your fist at shoulder level, the way boxers do, to protect your head. Then punch straight out from your shoulder. Your nonpunching hand should guard your jaw or the middle section.

REVERSE PUNCH

The reverse punch *(gyaku-tsuki)* generates more power than any other punch, so it is used almost exclusively in sparring. The reverse punch is performed in exactly the same way as the straight punch. The only difference is in the placement of your feet. When you punch with the hand that is on the same side as your front leg, you are throwing a straight punch. When punching from the same side as your back leg, you are executing a reverse punch. You are usually able to generate more power with a reverse punch because of your body position. You can pivot your hips into the punch to get the full force of your body behind it.

Sparring Tip Like boxers, many Karate practitioners use a straight punch to feel out their opponent, then when they find an opening, follow up with a powerful reverse punch. Practice this technique using a heavy bag before putting it into play in practice sparring.

DOUBLE PUNCH

Double punches *(ren-tsuki)* are accomplished by quickly punching several times in a row, alternating punching hands. This can be practiced on a heavy bag or speed bag. Remember to put your body weight behind each punch instead of simply throwing your hands forward. As the first punch lands, launch the second punch (photos a-b). The first hand should come back to protect your jaw or midsection. Continue in this way for four or five strikes in a row.

In sparring, the technique can be used while stepping forward. With each step, perform a reverse punch. This helps a fighter get "inside" while possibly scoring a point. It can also count as a full point if the opponent doesn't defend several punches in a row.

Intermediate and Advanced Hand Techniques

Karate practitioners use a variety of hand techniques to score points in sparring. Remember that in some tournaments, open hand techniques to the face are not legal. Doing two hand techniques in a row is an effective way to score on an opponent. For example, if you perform a knife hand strike with your right hand, follow it immediately with a knife hand strike with your left hand. This way, the strike with your right hand will draw the block, allowing you to score to an unguarded target with your left hand.

KNIFE HAND STRIKE

Knife hand strikes *(shuto-uchi)* use the outer edge of your open hand (the little finger edge) as the striking surface. To position your hand correctly, keep all your fingers and your thumb straight. Keep your wrist straight and your hand and fingers tight. The basic knife hand strike is chambered, palm up, near the opposite side shoulder. Then, sweep your hand across your body, straightening your elbow as you go. As you reach your target, twist your wrist so that your palm faces down.

This adds power to the technique. The hand that you are not striking with should remain a fist at your side. By extending this fist slightly forward and then pulling it back as you strike, you can create the punch (strike)/pull movement necessary for the correct execution of the technique.

You can also chamber the knife hand at the same side shoulder. In this case, the palm is up and remains in that position as you sweep the hand toward the target. This variation is faster and more direct, so it is more likely to score during sparring.

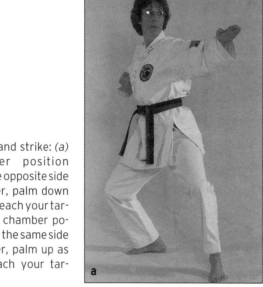 

Knife hand strike: *(a)* chamber position near the opposite side shoulder, palm down as you reach your target, *(b)* chamber position at the same side shoulder, palm up as you reach your target.

RIDGE HAND STRIKE

The ridge hand strike *(haito)* uses the inner edge of your hand (the thumb edge) as the striking surface. To make a ridge hand, start with your hand in the knife hand position, then fold your thumb under your hand. The thumb edge of your hand should be smooth. Start with your ridge hand extended out to the side, parallel to the ground. Quickly sweep your arm across your body, pivoting at the waist and hips as you do so. Strike the target with the inner edge of your hand.

Sparring Tip Performing this technique can leave your chest open, which makes it a vulnerable target area. Practice the ridge hand strike while keeping your body turned away from your opponent to avoid this problem.

REVERSE RIDGE HAND STRIKE

This is a variation of the ridge hand strike. With your ridge hand held under the opposite arm, palm down, sweep your arm outward across your body, keeping your elbow slightly bent. At the moment of impact, twist your wrist so that your palm faces up. Strike with the thumb edge of your hand. This technique keeps your chest protected until the last possible moment, so it is often used in sparring in place of the ridge hand strike.

PALM STRIKE

The palm strike *(teisho)* is performed like a punch, except that the hand remains open. The heel of the hand is the striking surface. Position your hand as for a knife hand strike, but with the fingers pulled slightly back and the heel of your hand forward. Chamber your hand on the same side, with fingers pointing down and palm facing forward. Strike forward with your hand, twisting your wrist at the moment of impact so that your fingers point up, but the heel of your hand is still forward. This technique is sometimes illegal in competition. It is sometimes restricted to the middle section.

A reverse palm strike is a variation of the palm strike. Instead of striking with the hand on the same side as the forward leg, you strike with the hand on the same side as the back leg.

The palm strike can be used in sparring to "push" the opponent away. This allows you to move out of punching range. Combined with a front kick (see the next section), it can be a difficult combination to block or counter.

SPEAR HAND STRIKE

The spear hand technique *(nukite)*, sometimes called spear fingers, uses the tips of the fingers as the striking surface. Position the hand in the knife hand position. The tips of the fingers should be held even with each other. You can bend your thumb at the knuckle to help strengthen the spear hand position. Your fingers must be kept strong so that they won't bend under impact.

With your fingers in the spear hand position, chamber your hand palm up and strike forward with your hand, fingers aiming for the target. Turn your palm down at the moment of impact. The tips of your fingers should thrust into your target.

Sparring Tip This technique is rarely used in sparring, but one effective tactic is to use it as a jab. It can be used for feinting and requires less commitment than a punch. Simply move your open hand slightly toward your target to see what happens and then take advantage of any opening.

BACKFIST STRIKE

The backfist strike *(uraken)* uses the back of the fist as the striking surface. This technique is usually reserved for the opponent's head. Chamber your fist near the opposite shoulder, with the palm facing outward. Sweep outward from your body, twisting your wrist at the moment of impact so that the back of your fist strikes the target area.

This technique is useful in sparring to strike quickly at your opponent's unguarded head. It can also be used in combination with a kick or punch to the middle section, which will draw the opponent's guard down, allowing the backfist to strike unblocked to the head. It can also be used to travel short distances effectively (it doesn't have to be chambered at the shoulder to be used in sparring).

DOWNWARD HAMMER FIST STRIKE

The hammer fist strike *(kentsui)*, also called the bottom fist strike, uses the bottom of the hand as the striking surface. Make your hand into a fist, as for a punch. Then, chamber your hand above the same side shoulder, with the bottom of your hand facing up and out. Sweep your hand down, making an arc so that the bottom of your fist strikes the target. This downward strike is only used when striking from above a target area. The key to an effective hammer fist strike is to use a circular motion, which generates speed and power.

Sparring Tip The downward hammer fist strike is most useful when performed after you've swept or thrown your opponent and are following up with a strike.

HORIZONTAL HAMMER FIST STRIKE

A variation of the hammer fist strike is the horizontal hammer fist strike. This begins chambered at the opposite shoulder and sweeps outward across the body. It is more useful in sparring than the downward hammer fist strike. However, it can be confused with a block, therefore earning no score, so use it mostly to set up other hand techniques.

Hand Striking Fundamentals

Although there are many hand striking techniques in the Karate sparring arsenal, some basic elements are common to all of them. Understanding and mastering these elements will make all of your hand striking techniques more effective.

Using the Correct Striking Surface

Hand striking with the correct surface is essential. Each hand strike uses a different surface. In each case, you should hold your wrist straight so that your hand stays on the same plane as your forearm.

The best way to ensure that you are striking with the correct surface is to use a striking post, which is simply an upright piece of wood, sometimes covered with material to prevent cuts, that has been secured to the floor or the ground. By striking the post, you can tell what striking surface you are using on your hand. If a striking post is not available, use any flat surface, such as a wall. A heavy bag or punching bag won't necessarily help you identify the correct striking surface. If all else fails, ask a partner to hold out a palm for you to strike against. This also gives you the "feel" you need to learn how to deliver your hand strikes.

Practice the hand technique slowly, extending your arm out until the striking surface touches the wall. In the reverse punch, for instance, only the first two knuckles should make contact with the surface. Adjust your fist and the way you hold your hand and arm until you are striking with the correct striking surface.

Martial artists sometimes bend or roll their wrists when they strike. This can cause sprains or tears and reduces the power of the punch. Practice striking a striking post or heavy bag to build your wrist strength. Wrist wraps or special bag gloves can help you keep your wrists steady until you've strengthened your wrist and arm muscles sufficiently. An old martial arts exercise for strengthening wrists is knuckle push-ups, as described on page 73.

Applying the Chamber and Twist

Mastering the chamber position and the wrist twist is crucial to achieving correct hand technique. Make sure your arm and hand are held in the correct chamber position for the technique. The twist at the end of the strike is also extremely important since it helps generate explosive power at the point of impact. Because almost all Karate hand and arm techniques, including strikes and blocks, require a twist at the end, it is an important part of the technique to practice.

Adopting the Strike/Pull Technique

To generate more power, instead of simply striking forward with your striking hand, you can also pull back with your nonstriking hand. This strike/pull technique helps you put your entire body behind a hand strike. Assume a comfortable fighting stance and chamber both hands at your waist. Reach forward slightly with your nonstriking hand (which should be made into a fist). As you strike with your striking hand, pull your outstretched nonstriking hand back to your side, returning it to the chamber position with the palm up (photo a). Leave your striking hand out in front. Then strike forward with your back hand, pulling your front hand to your side as you do so (photo b). With some repetition, this will come naturally and will improve the power of your strikes. It's also a skill that can be built on later. For instance, you may reach forward and grab your opponent with your back hand, pulling him or her toward you as you strike forward. This increases the impact of the technique.

Increase the power of your punches by pivoting your hips forward as you strike.

Generating Power

Many martial artists use only their arms from the shoulder down to generate power in their hand techniques, resulting in a less powerful strike. A related problem occurs when martial artists overextend their arms. Sometimes a martial artist tries to add power to a punch or striking technique by throwing the arm so far forward that the shoulder also rolls forward. For best effect, your shoulder should always stay on the same plane as your chest. Don't let your shoulder roll forward beyond your chest.

To generate more power, instead of overextending your arm, put your whole body behind your strike. This is done by using your hips to move your body back and forth.

To understand how this works, stand in an open leg stance. Chamber your fist at your side. As you punch forward, twist the same side hip forward as well. You should notice a difference in the power of your strikes. You can also step or slide into a punch to add power. Practice this by stepping forward and striking at the same time. Combine the step and the hip pivot at the same time to significantly increase the power of your punches.

Using a Punching Bag

By using a punching bag, a heavy bag, or another solid target, you can better measure the power of your punches. Use bag gloves or sparring equipment, especially if you haven't been doing much bag work. Use the hip pivot and the step forward while working on hand striking techniques on the heavy bag. You may be surprised at how rapidly your hand striking techniques improve. To get the most from these suggestions, practice for several minutes on the heavy bag each day. This will also strengthen your arms and wrists to eliminate wrist rolls.

Improving Upper Body Fitness

Upper body strength is essential to explosive hand techniques. You can lift weights to achieve this strength, but you can also build considerable upper body strength just by performing push-ups. Start with 10 or 20 repetitions of the basic push-up and go from there. Lie flat on the floor and place your palms directly under your shoulders. Keep your abdomen tight and your body straight, and push up. If these are difficult to do at first, rest your knees on the floor. Your goal, either short or long term depending on your physical condition, should be to perform 75 push-ups in a row, resting only your palms and toes on the floor.

By changing the placement of your hands, you can vary the push-ups and their physical effects. Try spreading your hands so they are extended two shoulder widths apart to work more of the chest muscles and biceps. You can bring your hands in close under your sternum to work your triceps. Finally, you can do knuckle push-ups. These are done by making your hands into fists and resting your weight on the first two knuckles of each hand (your punching knuckles). Knuckle push-ups strengthen your wrists and forearms to help produce more powerful punches.

If you have access to a pull-up bar (sometimes called a chin-up bar), work on pull-ups. If you can't do these at first, have a friend act as spotter. Grip the bar with your hands placed about shoulder-width apart and pull straight up. By changing the grip you have on the bar, you can vary the pull-up. A wide grip works the triceps and shoulders; a reverse grip works the biceps.

Kicking Techniques

While hand striking techniques are more effective when the opponent is closer, kicking techniques, which use any part of the foot as the striking surface, are most effective when the opponent is several feet away. Although high kicks are allowed in most Karate competition, middle kicks are used much more often.

Kicking techniques can be performed with either the front or back leg. From a back or fighting stance, for example, you can do a side kick with either your forward leg or your back leg. The only difference is how you shift your weight. A front leg side kick requires you to move your weight to the back leg as you kick, whereas a back leg side kick requires you to move your weight to the front leg.

Although front and back leg kicks are executed basically in the same way, they have different purposes. The front leg kick is always the faster kick, and the back leg kick is always the more powerful. Which you use will depend on circumstances. The faster kick might distract an opponent, whereas the more powerful kick might score a point. As you learn more about Karate sparring, it will become easier to judge when to use which kick. While you will find that some kicks suit your abilities better than others, you should be sure to practice all kicks.

Basic Kicks

Although Karate practitioners rely on hand techniques as much or more than kicking techniques, mastering the basic kicks is essential to excellent Karate sparring. Most practitioners learn the basic kicks within the first few months of training, but it can take years to master them. Even when you've moved on to flashier techniques, remember that your basic kicks are essential to success in sparring, so keep practicing and perfecting them.

FRONT KICK

The front kick *(mae-geri)* strikes directly to the front, usually to the middle section. The striking surface is the ball of your foot. Position your foot by pointing your foot and pulling your toes back. Lift your kicking leg high, bending your knee at a 90-degree angle. Your leg should be slightly in front of your body. From this tight chamber position, snap your leg forward, striking with the ball of your foot. An advanced technique is to raise the heel of your back foot during the kick.

The front kick can emphasize different movements. The snap front kick is performed with a sharp whipping movement and has the advantage of speed. The push or thrust front kick, which uses the whole foot, is performed by pushing the target away with the foot. Its advantage is power. The instep front kick, which uses the instep as the striking surface, is used to kick upward into the groin. In most sparring competitions, techniques to the groin are illegal, so the instep kick should be avoided.

The front kick is a quick kick that can be used to stop an opponent who charges in. Chamber the foot and thrust forward to stop the opponent, then follow up with a hand technique to score a point.

CRESCENT KICKS

Crescent kicks (*makazuki-geri*) use either the inner or the outer edge of the foot as the striking surface, depending on the direction the kick travels. There are two kinds of crescent kicks: inside-outside (uses the outer edge) and outside-inside (uses the inner edge).

In a crescent kick, the kicking leg travels in an arc, moving across the body. The leg is swung up as high as possible, then brought down quickly.

Inside-Outside Crescent Kick

Lift your kicking leg from the ground. Sweep it forward, coming slightly across your body (photo a). Swing your leg as far upward as you can and sweep to the side in a circular movement (photo b). This is the actual strike. The outer edge of the foot is the striking surface and should be used to strike a high target area. Finish the kick by landing with your foot in the same position it started from. In Karate sparring, the shoulder is not a legal target area, so be certain to strike to the side of the head instead of landing the leg on your opponent's shoulder.

Sparring Tip Because this kick sweeps across a large area before landing, the opponent can sometimes see it coming and block or evade it. To avoid this problem, try chambering the kick as you would a front kick, then flick the kick out and sweep over to strike with the outer edge of your foot. This can fool your opponent into expecting a front kick, therefore leaving the side of his or her chest or head open.

Outside-Inside Crescent Kick

Lift your kicking leg from the ground. Sweep to the side, bringing your leg as high up as possible (photo a, page 76). Pull your leg slightly across your body. This is the actual strike, and the inner edge of the foot is the striking surface (photo b, page 76). Finish by landing with your foot in the same position it started from. This kick is usually used to kick to the high section. Be certain not to drop it on your opponent's shoulder, because that is not a legal target area.

Outside-inside crescent kick.

Sparring Tip Because the crescent kick can sometimes be anticipated by the opponent, use it in combination with another technique. For instance, if you punch with the arm on the opposite side, then immediately launch an outside-inside crescent kick, your opponent will attempt to block or evade the punch but will not see the kick coming and so it can land unblocked.

SIDE KICK

The side kick (*yoko-geri*) uses the bottom of your heel and the outer or knife edge of your foot to strike. Your target is directly in front of you, but you pivot so that your side faces the target before you deliver the strike.

Cock your kicking leg so that your knee is bent at least 90 degrees. Keep your foot tight by making it parallel to the floor. The higher and tighter this chamber position, the more powerful the kick. Pivot on your supporting foot 180 degrees so that your toes point away from the target. Snap your kicking leg out, extending your knee. Lean slightly over your supporting leg to maintain your balance. Strike your target with the heel of your foot. By keeping the toes of your striking foot either parallel to the floor or turned slightly downward, you will be more likely to strike your target correctly. Striking with your toes pointing up signals incorrect technique and can actually cause injury to your ankle or hip.

Either a front leg or back leg side kick can be used. The front leg kick is faster, but the back leg kick is more powerful.

The side kick can be used to feint in sparring. Chamber the leg high and tight and jab toward the opponent in quick movements. The opponent may commit to a technique that you can counter. Or use the side kick as a jab and when you see an opening, immediately follow with a hand technique such as a reverse punch or a ridge hand strike.

ROUNDHOUSE KICK

The roundhouse kick *(mawashi-geri)* strikes a target in front of you, but the kick comes from the side, moving in an arc from outside to inside. The striking surface is the top of the foot, the instep. Lift your kicking leg from the ground and bring it in an arc from the side to the front. Your knee should be bent 90 degrees and it should face your target. Your supporting foot should pivot 180 degrees so that your toes point away from the target. As you bring your kicking leg around, the side of your leg should be parallel to the ground. Sweeping forward, snap your foot out, striking the target with your instep. Your foot should be kept pointed and tight to absorb the impact of the strike.

The thrust roundhouse kick is done by thrusting the hips out as the kick lands, to add power. The supporting foot pivots slightly more than usual for this powerful technique.

Roundhouse kicks can be done with the front leg or the back leg. Keep in mind, though, that back leg kicks are also more easily countered by opponents.

A short roundhouse kick moves in a straight line to the target instead of moving in an arc or semicircle toward the target. Although less powerful than a traditional roundhouse kick, it is faster. It is chambered like a side kick, but the knee acts as a hinge, sweeping the foot toward the target. Advanced practitioners often use it to confuse their opponents. The opponent expects a side kick and may not be prepared to counter a roundhouse kick.

BACK KICK

The back kick *(ushiro-geri)* is similar to a side kick in that your leg chambers the same way and the striking surface of the foot is the same (heel and knife edge). The difference is that your body makes a complete revolution while striking.

Stand in a fighting stance. The foot closest to the target is the pivot foot. Lift the leg farthest from the target, chambering it tightly as you would for a side kick. Bend the knee at least 90 degrees. Instead of pivoting to the front and kicking, however, turn to the back. Lean over your supporting foot to maintain your balance. Your kicking leg should be horizontal to the floor. As soon as your back is to the target, strike with your foot. Then rechamber the kick and return to your starting position. You will have made a complete 360-degree revolution. This type of kick is extremely powerful and makes a good countering technique. It is usually not a good lead-off or attacking technique since it can be anticipated by the opponent.

Sparring Tip In sparring, use a modified version of this kick. Turn to the back and strike your target, but instead of rechambering and returning to your starting position, rechamber and kick with a side kick. This way, even if your opponent blocks or evades the back kick, you will be able to score a point with the side kick. You can also do two back kicks in a row using this technique.

Intermediate and Advanced Kicks

In Karate, the intermediate and advanced kicks aren't different from the basic kicks; they are simply different ways of approaching the basic kicks. For this reason, it is essential that you master the basic kicks before moving on. In sparring, close to 90 percent of all kicks will be basic kicks with only a few of the more advanced kicks used to add variety.

JUMP KICKS

Many kicks can be performed with a jump. The side kick, for example, can travel a considerable distance if you jump while performing it. To perform a jump side kick, move your supporting leg in so that it almost touches the foot of your kicking leg. Chamber your kicking leg by picking it up high and cocking the knee 90 degrees. Kick straight out to the side. No turning is necessary. As you become more proficient with the technique, you will jump as you move your supporting leg so that both feet are off the ground at the same time. Then, you will strike out with your kick, rechamber, and land.

You can also add a jump to a front kick or a roundhouse kick. This is done by standing with your feet close together, facing the target. Crouch so that your knees bend about 45 degrees. The rest of your body should remain upright. Spring from the crouch, jumping into the air. As your feet leave the ground, chamber your leg and kick out, using the ball of your foot for a front kick and the instep of your foot for a roundhouse kick.

You can also add a jump to the back kick. This is done by facing the target with your knees bent slightly. As you jump, chamber your back leg, rotate, and kick the target with your heel. Return to the starting position.

Jumping kicks are not used very often in Karate sparring. The best time to use them is when you need to travel a great distance, in which case a jump side kick can help you close the gap; when you want to score to the high section, in which case the jump front kick could score; or when you want to demonstrate power, in which case the jump reverse kick to the midsection would certainly show good power.

Jump side kick.

Jump roundhouse kick.

Jump back kick.

Jump front kick.

The best way to work on a jump kick is to break it into its various parts. Practice jumping first without worrying about the kick. Then put the jump and the kick together, going slowly at first, then faster as you become better at it. Each jump kick has a slightly different jump, but as you master each jump, the others become easier.

Sparring Tip Very few jump kicks are used in sparring with the exception of the jump back kick. This technique allows you to generate more power or to cover more distance than a regular back kick and can be used very effectively as a countering technique. Rarely should it be used to set up an attack.

STEP KICK

A step kick is simply a kick with a step added to it. Your supporting leg steps and lands next to your kicking foot (photos a-b). Your kicking leg chambers and strikes almost immediately (photo c). If you are sparring someone who is out of your kicking range, you can step and deliver a kick quickly.

DOUBLE KICK

One of the best ways to catch your opponent off guard is to use a double kick, which means simply striking with a kick and then, without setting your foot down, striking again. A double roundhouse kick, then, would be two roundhouse kicks in a row without putting your foot down. This is an especially valuable technique if you vary your target area. The first kick, for instance, might be aimed at the middle section (photo a) while the second is aimed at the high section (photo b). This makes it impossible for your opponent to anticipate where to block.

The double kick can also make use of two different kinds of kicks. A side kick to the ribs may be followed by a roundhouse kick to the head. Since the roundhouse kick is coming at a slightly different angle than that of the side kick, even if your opponent is anticipating a double kick, he or she likely won't be able to block it.

Any direct kick, such as a front kick, side kick, roundhouse kick, or even back kick, can be made into a double kick. However, circular kicks, such as crescent kicks, cannot be done this way.

Sparring Tip The more kicks you can do in a row without setting your leg down, the more likely you will be to draw your opponent into making a mistake. Practice the balance you need and build the necessary strength by holding your leg in the chamber position for a few minutes at a time, then striking repeatedly with your leg, then holding it in the chamber position, and so on.

Kicking Fundamentals

As with all striking techniques, the most essential element to effective kicking is to kick with confidence. Although your kick may not be perfect, a confident kick can make up for many mistakes. Nevertheless, it is important to perfect your kicks with slow practice. Work on correctly chambering, pivoting, striking with the appropriate part of the foot, rechambering, and returning to the original position. Practice each kick at least 10 times on each leg at each workout session.

Chambering and Rechambering

Two elements are essential to strong kicks in sparring: the chamber and the rechamber. Even though each kick has a slightly different chamber position, all chambers should be high and tight, which means the leg should rise as far as you can make it go and the bend at the knee should be sharp and strong. Even if you are kicking to a middle target area, a high and tight chamber is necessary for good power and proper technique. A high and tight chamber will also help you to kick to high target areas even if your flexibility needs work.

Rechambering your kick after you have successfully completed your strike is important in sparring. This leaves you in a position to kick again quickly if you need to. If you rechamber quickly after striking, you can easily use your leg to block your opponent's attacks.

Some Karate practitioners work on making the chambers for all their kicks look the same so that a sparring opponent cannot guess which kick is going to be used. The fighter can decide at the last second, depending on what the opponent is doing. The legendary Karate fighter Bill Wallace used this technique to excellent effect, winning many sparring titles even though he could only kick with one leg (the other was badly injured and couldn't be used to strike).

Kicking Essentials

1. Chamber.
2. Pivot (on the supporting foot).
3. Strike (with the correct striking surface).
4. Rechamber (foot shouldn't drop at end of strike).
5. Return (to your starting position).

Speeding Up Your Kicks

Speed in kicking keeps you agile and ready for your next move. If your kicks are too slow, your opponent can easily see them coming and can counter or avoid them. Even more dangerous, your opponent could grab your leg and throw you if you are too slow. For this reason, working on speed is essential.

One way to improve speed is to add a whipping or snapping motion at the end of the kick. Instead of sweeping or pushing with your kick, try to snap it at the moment of impact. This sharp snap generates speed and power, just the way snapping a whip works.

A good way to get the necessary snap at the end of your kick is to kick forward as quickly as possible and then return your leg to the chamber position faster than you kicked. This requires you to work on kicking forward and pulling your kick back instead of relying on momentum. In addition to increasing your kicking speed, this technique will also build strength.

Elbow and Knee Strikes

Karate fighters can often use elbow and knee strikes during sparring. These techniques work in close range, especially if you're in too close for effective hand techniques. Some of these techniques can travel—that is, cover quite a distance—so they can also be used to get into fighting range.

Elbow Strikes

The two striking areas on the elbow are the front of the elbow and the point of the elbow. Every elbow strike *(empi-ate)* uses one or the other of these striking surfaces.

FORWARD ELBOW STRIKE

The forward elbow strike uses the front of the elbow as the striking surface. For the forward elbow strike, the target is directly in front of you. Bend the striking arm tightly. Keep your arm parallel to the floor. Pivoting at the waist, turn slightly to the back, reaching behind you with the elbow. Then uncoil at the waist, sweeping your elbow forward and through the target.

In sparring, the elbow strike is most effective when targeted to the high section. The technique is more likely to be seen and judged as a score this way.

REVERSE ELBOW STRIKE

The reverse elbow strike uses the point of the elbow as the striking surface. The target is directly behind you. Bend your arm so that it is cocked at a 90-degree angle. Your forearm and fist should be parallel to the floor. Reach forward slightly with your arm to generate more power, then shove backward using the palm of your opposing hand to help push. The point of your elbow should drive backward, striking the target.

You can cover distance using this technique by sliding backward as you execute the elbow strike. It can catch an opponent off guard, particularly if he or she tends to circle. However, this technique is rarely used in sparring.

UPWARD ELBOW STRIKE

The upward elbow strike uses the front of the elbow as the striking surface. Bend your striking arm tightly so that the point of your elbow faces toward the floor. Your hand should be a fist. Reach back slightly with your elbow, then sweep the elbow upward. As you strike, your fist should be at the side of your head near your ear.

This technique can be used against the underside of a target. In sparring, it can be effective as a strike to the head or chin, but be careful not to make contact with the throat.

DOWNWARD ELBOW STRIKE

This technique uses the point of the elbow as the striking surface. Bend your arm so that it makes a 90-degree angle. Your upper arm should be parallel to the floor; your hand should be a fist. Reach up slightly with your arm, then drive directly downward through the target, striking with the point of your elbow.

In sparring competition, this technique can be used when the opponent has been swept or thrown and you are following up with a strike. A pronounced downward elbow strike after a takedown technique meets the criterion for following up throws.

SIDE ELBOW STRIKE

The side elbow strike uses the point of the elbow as the striking surface. The target is to the side. Bend your striking arm so that it is cocked at a 90-degree angle. Your hand should be a fist. Bring your arm slightly across your body. Drive your elbow to the side, thrusting the point of your elbow into the target. You can use the palm of the opposite hand to help push the arm through.

To increase the distance of this technique, you can step or slide to the side as you perform it. This technique is rarely used in sparring, but it can effectively surprise an opponent, especially one who is circling around you.

Knee Strikes

Knee strikes are very straightforward techniques. You simply strike the target with your knee. You can increase the power of knee strikes by pulling the target toward your knee while driving your knee into it. In sparring, you can grasp your opponent's uniform and pull him or her into your knee in order to score.

STRAIGHT KNEE STRIKE

The straight knee strike uses the front of the kneecap as the striking surface. Swing your striking leg forward, bending your knee to a 90-degree angle. Drive the knee directly into the target. This strike works for middle section and high section. (It can also be used to strike to the groin, but not in competition.) To knee strike to the face, it helps to grab the opponent's uniform near the shoulders and pull down toward your knee as you strike.

This technique can be used when you are in too close to your opponent for a kicking technique to be used. Use a hand technique, such as a ridge hand strike, to set it up, then pull the opponent into your knee.

ROUNDHOUSE KNEE STRIKE

Like the roundhouse kick, the roundhouse knee strike approaches from the side. Lift your striking leg from the floor. Bend the knee at a 45-degree angle, keeping the inner side of the leg turned toward the floor. Sweep from the side across your body and drive your knee into the target. You can grab your opponent's uniform and pull him or her toward you to score a point in sparring.

Sparring Tip Use knee strikes in combination with the roundhouse kick. First, strike with several roundhouse kicks (it doesn't matter if they score or not). Then, the next time you chamber for a roundhouse kick, this is what your opponent will expect. Instead, deliver the knee strike to score a point.

Elbow and Knee Strike Fundamentals

To improve your knee and elbow strikes, think speed. Martial artists commonly try to push or thrust when striking with their elbows and knees. They assume that using power will make the technique effective. But these strikes rely on speed. Strike as quickly as possible and return to the starting position, prepared to strike again.

For maximum effect, try to return to the starting position faster than you struck. Think of delivering a stinging blow as opposed to a crushing blow. Moving quickly makes it harder for your opponent to counter or catch you off guard.

Takedown Techniques

Sweeps, takedowns, and throws are exciting but dangerous techniques in Karate. Always practice takedown techniques in a safe place with a padded mat. Make sure your practice partner understands which direction he or she is going to fall and where you are going to attack. This helps prevent accidental injuries. Never drop someone that you are throwing (not even in competition). Always hold on to your partners/opponents, helping them down. It is courteous to help them back up again.

Falling Correctly

Takedown techniques can cause injury if you don't know how to fall. Most people instinctively put a hand out to break a fall. However, this is a good way to hurt yourself.

Forward breakfall.

On throws to the front, avoid landing on or hitting your face. However, don't spare your face by falling directly on your hand. Keep your head lifted and your face turned to the side. Thrust an arm and shoulder forward to absorb the impact. Instead of landing directly on your hand, reach forward with it, bending at the elbow. Slide yourself forward as you fall.

Backward breakfall.

Falls to the back should be absorbed with your hip and shoulder. Your head should never touch the ground. Tuck your chin tightly to your chest. Don't extend your arm straight out to the back to catch yourself. This can easily cause an impact injury to your hand or arm. Land first on your hip and shoulder, then slap your hand, palm down, on the ground, extending your arm to stop the momentum of the fall.

Takedowns Countering Hand Strikes

Most takedown techniques are counters to punches or hand strikes. Since many hand techniques are used in Karate, learning to counter them with takedown techniques can improve your sparring tremendously.

SHOULDER TAKEDOWN

When the opponent strikes, step away from the punch (or hand strike) toward the opponent's body. With your nearest hand, block the punch and grab the wrist of the opponent's punching hand (photo a). Grab the shoulder of the punching arm with your other hand. Slide your closest foot behind the opponent's leg (photo b). Push on the shoulder and hook the opponent's leg out from under. Throw him or her to the ground (photo c).

Sparring Tip Set up this takedown by getting your opponent to throw a punch or other hand technique. The best way to do this is to perform one or two hand techniques of your own and get into hand range (as opposed to kicking range). This will almost always force your opponent to resort to a hand technique. Since you know it's coming, you'll be ready for the takedown.

ELBOW TAKEDOWN

When the opponent strikes, step away from the punch (or hand strike) toward the opponent's body. With your nearest hand, block and grab the wrist of the opponent's punching hand. With your free hand, grab the opponent's elbow (photo a). Position your fingers into the joint. Bend the opponent's elbow, keeping the elbow tightly bent. Then, slide your nearest foot behind the opponent's foot (photo b). Pull up on the opponent's elbow. This should off-balance your opponent. Hook his or her leg out from under. Throw him or her to the ground (photo c).

HIP THROW

When the opponent strikes, block with your outside arm as you rotate away from the punch (photo a). Your back should face the opponent's body and your feet should straddle your opponent's nearest foot. Next, deliver a backward elbow strike into the opponent's solar plexus. Reach behind you. Grab the opponent's upper arm and shoulder (or the uniform). Uncoil and pull the opponent against your hip, using it as a pivot point. Throw the opponent over your hip (photo b).

Sparring Tip Use this technique in connection with a back kick. When your opponent launches a reverse punch or a roundhouse kick, perform a back kick. Instead of rechambering and returning to your starting position, kick and set your foot down so that your back or side is toward the opponent, then perform the takedown.

Takedowns Countering Kicks

Using a takedown technique as a counter to a kick can be dangerous (to both fighters) except under certain circumstances. When a takedown is used to counter a punch or hand strike, the opponent's attack can be avoided or deflected and the takedown performed with little danger to either partner. However, if a kick is coming straight at you and you avoid or deflect it, you won't be in any position to perform a takedown technique. You will be at kicking distance, which is too far away. If you don't block or counter the kick, but instead try to perform a takedown immediately, you can easily be struck. Bottom line: takedowns countering kicks are difficult to do.

The exception to this general rule is for kicks that come from the side instead of from straight ahead. This includes roundhouse kicks, crescent kicks, and spinning wheel kicks, all of which can be countered with a throw. Since the spinning wheel kick is rarely used in competition, its countering throw doesn't need to be practiced. If you want to try, the technique is the same as for the takedown countering a roundhouse kick or crescent kick.

TAKEDOWN COUNTERING ROUNDHOUSE KICK OR CRESCENT KICK

As your opponent performs the kick either to the middle section or the high section, block the technique with your hands or forearms. Then, step forward quickly, grab the opponent's uniform or shoulder (photo a). Then hook his or her supporting leg out from under, as in photo b.

This technique must be performed carefully; if you drop the opponent, you may be assessed a penalty for a dangerous throw.

Takedown Essentials

As with other Karate techniques, the essential element to successful takedowns is speed. The more quickly you execute the technique, the more likely you will be to succeed. Speed also makes it harder for the opponent to resist the throw. Practice the techniques slowly and carefully at first. As you build confidence, you can move more quickly (but still use caution). With practice, you will be able to guide your opponents' momentum and use their energy against them. This makes throws, takedowns, and sweeps easier to accomplish with less effort and power.

Defensive Techniques

In order to avoid your opponent's attacks, you should work on certain defensive techniques and maneuvers. These include blocks, which keep your opponent's techniques from landing on a target area, and body movements, which shift you out of the line of attack.

Blocks

Whenever you block during a sparring match, remember to keep one hand guarding your body, in position to guard your head, at all times. Fighters sometimes try to force you to block so that your body is unguarded or open, and then deliver the strike they originally intended. For this reason, you should perform most blocks with your forward arm, with your back arm in position to cover your body and head if necessary.

Basic Blocks

Two basic blocks are used in Karate sparring to protect the middle and the high section. Once these blocks are mastered, the fighter can add other defensive techniques to his or her arsenal.

DOWNWARD BLOCK

The downward block *(gedan barai-uke)* is used to deflect punches and kicks delivered to the middle or low section, using the inner surface of the arm as the blocking surface. To perform a downward block, make a fist with the hand of your blocking arm. Bring your blocking arm up to your opposite shoulder so that your palm faces the ceiling. With a sweeping motion, bring your arm down across your body, turning your wrist so that your palm faces the outside. Your arm should stop slightly beyond your knee. Keep your wrist and hand strong in case of contact with the kick or hand strike you are blocking.

The downward block is good for deflecting strikes to the middle section. It can be used to push the opponent's hand or foot away, off-balancing him or her and allowing you to set up a counter of your own.

UPPER BLOCK

The upper block *(jodan-uke)* is used to protect the head and shoulders. Bend the blocking arm so that the fist rests under your opposite arm, near the shoulder. Your palm faces down. Pulling your opposite arm back toward your side, sweep your blocking arm up, keeping your elbow cocked at a 45-degree angle. Your blocking arm should rise slightly above the top of your head. Twist your arm so that the palm of your hand and the inner surface of your arm face the ceiling. You should be able to see under your block. It should be strong enough to protect the top of your head from a downward strike.

Sparring Tip The upper block can protect against any strike to the head, but remember to use your nonblocking arm to guard your middle section or your chest will be exposed and open to any second strike your opponent may make.

Intermediate and Advanced Blocks

Although the downward and upper block can be used to ward off many Karate techniques, other blocking techniques are more effective, especially against certain types of techniques. Once the basic blocks are mastered, add the following blocks to your defensive techniques.

CRESCENT BLOCKS

These blocks protect the middle section of your body, including your ribs and your solar plexus. They are performed by making a sweeping motion in front of your body. A twisting motion at the end of the block helps deflect strikes. There are two kinds of crescent blocks: inside-outside blocks and outside-inside blocks, which are distinguished simply by the direction in which the block travels.

Inside-Outside Crescent Block

The inside-outside block *(uchi-ude-uke)* begins with your blocking arm, hand as a fist, under your opposite arm, as with an upper block. Keep your palm facing down and your arm parallel to the floor (photo a). Sweep your blocking arm out from your body so that it moves toward your forward leg. As it sweeps, your forearm and fist should rise so that they are perpendicular to the ground. The elbow should be bent at a 90-degree angle. Pull your opposite (nonblocking) arm back to your side, chambering your fist with the palm up (photo b). This will prepare you to punch or to execute another block. As your blocking arm crosses your forward leg, twist your forearm so that your palm faces you. This twist helps knock away the opponent's strike. This block will guard against any techniques aimed at the middle section, especially those that come from the side. It is very powerful and can move the opponent out of position, allowing you to counterattack.

Sparring Tip Use this block in combination with a counterattack. When the opponent strikes, block the strike with the inside-outside block. Since your block will move the opponent's arm or foot out of the way, you will have an unblocked target area. Immediately perform a hand striking technique with your other hand.

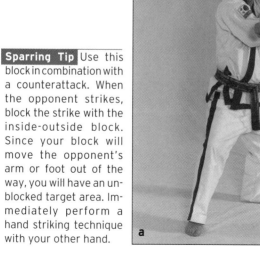

Outside-Inside Block

The outside-inside block *(soto-ude-uke)* is also done with the forward arm. Your nonblocking arm should guard your middle. Reach behind with your blocking arm, twisting at the waist, as shown in photo a. Your elbow should be cocked so that your upper arm is horizontal to the floor and your forearm and fist are perpendicular to it. Your palm faces forward. Your opposite arm, hand as a fist, is in front of your body. As you sweep with the blocking arm from back to front, pull your opposite arm back so that it rests chambered at your waist, palm up and ready to strike or block. Untwist or uncoil at the waist as you sweep with the blocking arm. This explosive movement adds power to your block. As your block sweeps across your forward leg, twist your wrist so that your palm faces you. Remember to keep your shoulder facing your target and your body facing away so that you are less vulnerable to a strike (photo b).

This block will guard against any technique aimed at the middle section, but it is particularly effective against strikes that come at an angle, such as the roundhouse kick.

FOOT AND LEG BLOCKS

You can use your feet and legs to block strikes as well. For example, a crescent kick can knock a punch or other hand technique aside. Or, drawing your leg up to protect your midsection can block a strike to that area. Occasionally, direct blocks to the leg are allowed in sparring. In this case, you simply use your foot to stop your opponent by pressing his or her leg away.

Work with a partner to sharpen your blocking skills.

Blocking Fundamentals

Blocks must be executed quickly and sharply. The momentum will help you deflect an attack. Make your blocks as powerful as your kicks and punches.

In most cases, you will be blocking with the most muscular (fleshy) part of your arm. In addition, you will perform a wrist twist at the end. Do not neglect the wrist or arm twist described for each block as it will help to deflect the strike.

Different blocks are used to block strikes from different directions and to guard different areas. To sharpen your skills, ask a partner to strike at any section of your body. Respond with a block appropriate to that section. If you don't have a partner, call out target areas (e.g., "head" or "chest") at random and then execute an appropriate block.

Sparring Tip Most blocks can be shortened in sparring so that they don't take as much time to complete. This makes them faster and more effective. While shortened blocks may not be as powerful, this is not as crucial in sparring as in, for instance, a self-defense situation. Also, by using shorter blocks, you will be committing less momentum to the block and will be less likely to leave a vulnerable target area open to a strike.

Other Defensive Maneuvers

As you practice the different blocks, you may decide that you need to incorporate other defensive techniques into your sparring as well. Blocking techniques have certain drawbacks. For instance, they require the same effort as a strike but can never score a point. They can be used by your opponent to draw off your guard so that he or she can strike to an unguarded area. The fighter ready for more finesse is ready for alternate defensive maneuvers.

Two of these are body shifting and footwork. Body shifting, which merely moves your body out of the line of attack, is an apparently simple method for avoiding attacks, but it requires practice. Footwork moves you into and out of different fighting ranges (kicking range, hand striking range, knee and elbow striking range, takedown range) and allows you to avoid attacks without physically blocking them. By not having to commit to a block, you have better control over the match. Footwork and body shifting also help you set up countering techniques, which will score points (blocks, of course, do not score points).

Body Shifting

The idea of body shifting is to get your body out of the way of an attack without expending a lot of effort moving or blocking. Practice body shifting by turning your chest away from oncoming strikes.

Have a partner punch or kick directly to your middle section. Simply pivot at the waist to avoid the strikes. Your partner can add a challenge by sometimes striking at your body and sometimes striking at your head.

CHANGING DIRECTION

Your opponent may sometimes circle around you, trying to find an opening. When you allow this without a challenge, you give control of the match to your opponent. When you resort to countering circling with circling, you're still relinquishing control of the match. In addition, some tournament judges consider this a rules infraction and may call a foul for it. To avoid these problems, meet circling by simply shifting your fighting stance position. As the circling opponent moves to the side or behind you, simply shift your direction.

To change direction in a fighting stance, merely turn your upper body from front to back (photos a-b). Shift your feet so they remain perpendicular to each other in this new direction. Your front foot should point forward; your back foot should point to the side. Redistribute your weight. By doing this, you will reserve your energy for attacking and defending. By not allowing your opponent's circling to get you out of your rhythm, you will be able to concentrate better on your strategy.

Footwork

As you spar, you're often unaware of where your feet are because your focus is on whether you'll be able to kick or punch in time to take advantage of an opening. Footwork proficiency, however, will allow you to move into and out of range effortlessly, and you'll be able to evade and counter your partner's techniques much more easily. It pays to spend time and effort on this.

After repeating each footwork pattern several times, ask a partner to punch or kick slowly while you perform a footwork pattern to evade or counter the technique. Speed up the practice as you become more competent.

FORWARD STEPPING

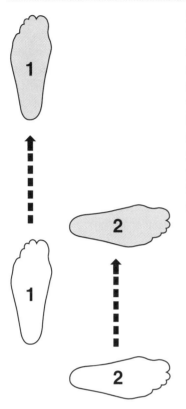

Forward stepping, also called straight stepping, helps you control the tempo of the match by allowing you to move into and out of different fighting ranges. It is also an excellent defensive technique. If your opponent is attacking with kicks that you are unable to counter, for example, use forward stepping to get into hand striking range where your opponent's kicks will be ineffective. Simply move directly toward your target. Slide your front foot forward, then pull your back foot forward. Practice small, quick slides toward your target. To vary forward stepping—and to avoid being attacked while moving in—perform a front kick with your front leg to slide forward, then put your front leg down without rechambering and slide your back foot forward. You will be in range as soon as your kick lands.

BACKWARD STEPPING

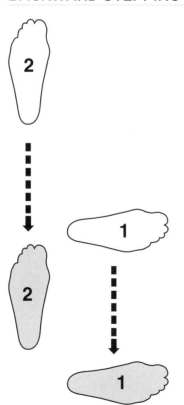

As a defensive maneuver, backward stepping will move you out of the range of your opponent. As an offensive maneuver, backward stepping will put you in the appropriate range for striking when you find yourself too close to use any techniques, or when you are in punching range and want to move to kicking range. Slide your back foot backward, then pull your front foot backward. Practice small, quick slides away from your target. To protect yourself, you can perform a front kick with your front leg, then set it down close to your back leg, then slide your back leg back into a fighting stance position.

You can combine forward stepping and backward stepping to move you into and out of fighting range. Practice the two together by making small, quick slides toward your target and then small, quick slides away from your target. The faster you can move your feet, the better a fighter you'll be.

SIDE STEPPING

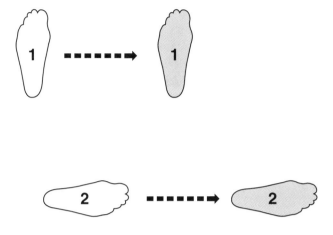

This technique is used to travel at a 90-degree angle to your opponent in order to move out of the way of a direct attack. By doing a quick side step, you are in a position to counter with your own technique. To step right, simply take a small step to the right with your left leg, away from your opponent. Your right leg should follow quickly. To move to the left, do the opposite, still leading with the left foot. You must move in the direction opposite the strike in order to evade it. Practice side stepping with a variety of techniques. Often, as your opponent moves forward with a technique, you can side step it and then kick or punch to your opponent's now-exposed ribs.

PIVOT STEPPING

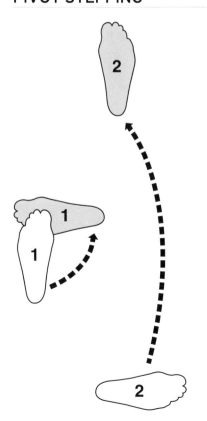

The pivot step is used to avoid any attack while you move toward or away from your opponent. To pivot step toward your opponent, push off with your rear foot and pivot in a circle on your front foot. Your opponent's attack will slide by you and you will be in a position to strike immediately. To pivot step away from your opponent, push off with your front foot and pivot in a circle on your back foot. Again, your opponent's attack will slide by you and you will be out of range of any further techniques. The pivot step can be especially helpful when your opponent is overwhelming you and you need a moment to regroup. Use it instead of turning your back on your opponent to avoid a strike, since this is illegal in competition and may result in a penalty.

CROSSOVER STEPPING

The crossover step allows you to cover a lot of ground while keeping your guard up. Bring your back foot over your front foot so that they cross. Then slide what is now your back foot forward toward your target. Your feet will be in the same position as they were originally, except that you'll be closer to your target. You can vary this technique by adding a kick to the end of it. To do this, bring your back foot over your front foot, then strike directly to the target with your back foot, using a side kick or a roundhouse kick.

Karate practitioners have a wide range of legal sparring techniques to choose from, with many offensive and defensive possibilities. Yet a surprising number of fighters rely on a few tried-and-true techniques. Improve your sparring by practicing and becoming comfortable with the entire range of Karate techniques available to you. Karate techniques build directly on the basics, however, so you must have mastery of the beginning techniques to move on to the intermediate and advanced techniques. Don't shortchange yourself; instead, practice the perfect execution of all techniques in order to become an unbeatable fighter.

CHAPTER 6
KARATE TACTICS

What one does is not as important as how and why one does it.

If your goal is to excel as a fighter, there is no substitute for practice. One of the best ways to gain competence and confidence with new techniques, sequences of techniques, and defensive maneuvers is through step sparring.

Step Sparring

Step sparring, a method of practicing fighting techniques in combination, takes place under more controlled circumstances than freestyle sparring. As such, it is a good way to prepare for the rigors of freestyle sparring. You can try out techniques you haven't used before, and you can put together different combinations of techniques to see if they work the way you expect them to. You can also improve your timing and countering skills. All of this is essential to freestyle sparring.

Step sparring is easiest if you work with a partner, but if you don't have one, you can practice shadow sparring or you can use a heavy bag as your partner. Simply imagine that an opponent is punching or kicking, and then respond. If you do use a partner, remember to use good control. In the beginning you should limit contact to light touch. As you and your partner gain confidence in your skills, you may agree to heavier contact, but special care should always be taken to avoid injury. Never exert full force when step sparring.

The Attack

To start, have your partner launch an attack with a single technique, like a punch to the chest or face. As you grow more proficient, vary the routine by having your partner attack with a variety of strikes to a variety of target areas.

The Block

In the beginner and early intermediate stages of sparring, respond to your partner's strike with a block. Begin with downward blocks and upper blocks, incorporating other blocks as you become more comfortable. In the more advanced stages, you will use more footwork and body shifting to stop an attack, relying less on blocks.

The Evasion

Blocking is time-consuming and commits you to a technique that can't score. As you advance in step sparring, you will rely more and more on evading an opponent's attacks. As you enter the later intermediate and advanced levels of step sparring, incorporate more body shifting and footwork techniques to avoid your opponent's attacks before launching your own attacks or countering techniques.

The Counter

After you have blocked or evaded your partner's strike, you should counter with two or three techniques that flow smoothly. Since you'll be starting from farther away and moving in, begin with kicking techniques and then move to hand techniques. Your partner should stay in place. (Having both partners moving back and forth is done in freestyle sparring, not step sparring).

When you have finished your series of techniques, *kiai* loudly to signal the end. Now it is your partner's turn to be on the defensive. Make sure the sessions are shared equally in turns of attacking and defending so that both partners gain valuable experience.

Step Sparring Drills

The following drills are intended to introduce you to step sparring. After you have gone through them several times and feel comfortable with each sequence, you can add your own variations. When you feel ready to strike out on your own, feel free to make up your own step sparring sequences.

When creating your own step sparring sequences, be sure to cover different kinds of punches, hand strikes, and kicks. The sequences you develop should suit your style, skills, and abilities. It is also important to think up several new sequences at every workout session rather than repeat the same sequences over and over. To do this, simply respond to your partner's attacks with a fresh series of techniques each time, trying to react to your partner's kicks or punches without thinking. This helps you learn to respond more quickly during actual sparring matches.

To make the step sparring scenario more realistic, both partners should signal that they are ready by giving a loud *kiai*. Once the signal is given, the attacker can wait for whatever length of time he or she wishes before attacking. The defending partner must wait for the attack instead of responding to the *kiai*. This builds timing skills and forces the defending partner to identify those subtle signals that indicate an attack is about to be launched. A signal might be a change in facial expression, a slight shift of feet, a shoulder moving forward. These are the very signals that superior fighters look for to anticipate attacks in competition.

For the following drills, the attacking partner should begin in a front stance. Body, including feet, should face the opponent. Feet should be about one and a half shoulder widths apart. The forward leg should have the knee bent at a 90-degree angle. The back leg should be extended back, the knee straight. Both feet should be flat on the floor. In step sparring, the attacking partner should begin in this stance with the left leg forward. He or she should perform a downward block over the left leg, then *kiai* to show readiness. The defending partner should stand naturally in an open leg ready stance. After hearing the attacking partner's *kiai*, the defending partner should also *kiai* to signal readiness. Then, the attacking partner should step forward with the right leg, at the same time performing a straight punch with the right hand. The straight punch should be aimed at the defender's chest or face.

Once the following drills have been learned and practiced thoroughly, change the attacking sequence. Use different stances and kicking techniques, and use both arms and legs.

COUNTER WITH HAND TECHNIQUES

As your partner punches to your face, side step to the right, away from the punch. Block the punch with your left hand as you step away. Deliver a knife hand or ridge hand strike to the high section, as shown in photo a. *Kiai* to signal the end of the sequence.

As a variation, after you perform the hand strike, step back and deliver a front kick to the midsection (photo b).

COUNTER WITH HAND STRIKE AND ELBOW STRIKE

As your partner punches to your face, side step right, away from the punch. Block the punch with your left hand as you step away. With your right hand, deliver a

knife hand or ridge hand strike to the high section (photo a, page 101). Then perform a forward elbow strike with your left arm (photo b). *Kiai* to signal the end of the sequence.

As a variation, after you perform the hand and elbow strikes, grab your partner's uniform, pulling him or her toward you and deliver a knee strike to the midsection, as shown in photo c.

COUNTER WITH DOUBLE KICK

As your partner punches to your face, step right, away from the punch. Block the punch with your left hand as you step away. Deliver a roundhouse kick to the high section (photo a). Without setting your leg down, rechamber and deliver a second kick to catch your opponent off guard (photos b and c). *Kiai* to signal the end of the sequence.

As a variation, use a front kick to the middle section. Or, using either round-house or front kicks, strike first to the middle section to draw your opponent's guard down, then strike to the high section without putting your leg down.

Another variation in this situation is to try using jump front and jump roundhouse kicks.

Freestyle Sparring Practice

While step sparring is a great way to introduce new techniques, counters, and defensive maneuvers into your repertoire, only through the practice of freestyle sparring will you become a proficient freestyle fighter. When you practice freestyle sparring, it is a good idea to keep tournament rules in mind. Although you should forget the rules every now and then and spar using every Karate technique you know, for the most part you should train for tournament rules. This means using techniques, strategies, and tactics that will succeed in tournament. Dust off those nontournament techniques—such as spinning techniques—every now and then for fun and skills enhancement.

When you don't have a partner to spar, you can still work on techniques such as body shifting or footwork. You can also invest in a heavy bag. Durable freestanding heavy bags, which you fill with water, make a good alternative to hanging a traditional heavy bag from a ceiling joist. Sparring a heavy bag is an excellent workout and offers the opportunity to work on offensive techniques.

Shadow sparring is also an effective way to practice offensive techniques. By sparring in front of a full-length mirror, you will learn how to do techniques better and more accurately.

Of course, nothing is as effective as good sparring partners to improve your sparring skills. Even if you are better than some of your sparring partners, remember that every martial artist you work with has something to teach you.

Maintaining Fighting Range

Fighting range is the most important concept a fighter can learn. The distance between you and your partner dictates the type of techniques you can do. Because each person has different arm and leg lengths and different reaches, fighting range is different for every person. Basically, if you are several feet from your partner, you are in kicking range and kicking techniques will be most effective. If you are within a foot or two of your partner, you are in punching range and punching or hand striking techniques will be most effective. If you are in closer than this, knee or elbow strikes, slightly modified, can be used. If you are too far from your partner for a kick to be effective, you are out of range and need to close the gap.

Beginning fighters often spar very far away from each other in order to avoid contact and because they don't have confidence in their control. Close the gap as you gain confidence.

Sometimes fighters get too close for any techniques to be effective. When this happens, back step—using a kick to guard—to move back into fighting range. Moving into and out of the different fighting ranges requires footwork, which was discussed in chapter 5 (see pages 95 to 98).

Fighting ranges: *(a)* kicking range, *(b)* punching range.

Fighting ranges: *(c)* knee and elbow striking range, and *(d)* out of range.

Assessing Your Strengths

An honest assessment of your strengths can go far in improving your sparring. First, consider your inherent physical abilities (not your Karate skills, which can improve quickly with practice). Are you quick? Agile? Powerful? Flexible? Pick techniques that match your physical abilities. Quick fighters should use front kicks, side kicks, and crescent kicks plus hand strikes such as knife hands and ridge hands. If you're a quick fighter, use front leg kicks instead of back leg kicks. Practice double kicks, which will add variety to your sparring.

Consider focusing on body shifting and footwork techniques to set up counters if you are an agile fighter. Any type of evasive movement will help you set up your opponents. Work on moving quickly into or out of fighting range, staying light on your feet. Agile fighters can often use takedown techniques to excellent effect.

If you are a powerful fighter, use direct, forcible techniques, such as punches, side kicks, and back kicks, plus elbow and knee strikes. Powerful fighters tend to be slower than other types of fighters, so you should focus on creating openings by setting up your opponent. Then you can anticipate the opening and strike powerfully. Grabbing and pulling your opponent toward you as you deliver a strike is an acceptable method of controlling quick and agile fighters, but remember to deliver a follow-up technique such as a knee strike right away, or you will be assessed a penalty.

Flexible fighters can take advantage of kicks. Although most Karate fighters concentrate on kicks to the midsection, fighters with a lot of leg flexibility can use higher kicks. Think of roundhouse kicks to the head. Flexible fighters can also use double kicks, especially middle-high combinations. Use your hands to set up your kicks. Punches to the midsection can draw your opponent's guard down, leaving him or her open to a high kick.

Assessing Your Strengths–Physical Abilities

Quick fighters: Use front kicks, side kicks, and crescent kicks plus hand strikes (knife hands, ridge hands). Use front leg kicks instead of back leg kicks. Double kicks will add variety to your sparring.

Agile fighters: Use body shifting and footwork techniques to set up counters. Move quickly into or out of fighting range. Use takedown techniques.

Powerful fighters: Use direct, forcible techniques (punches, side kicks, and back kicks, plus elbow and knee strikes). Create openings by setting up opponent. Grab and pull opponent forward to control quick and agile fighters.

Flexible fighters: Use kicks, especially to the high section. Double kicks can be effective, especially middle-high combinations. Use hands to set up kicks.

The next aspect to assess is your body type. Are you tall or short or average? Are you big, small, in-between? How you answer will help you devise suitable sparring strategies. For example, if you are short but big, you can deliver power blows, but your opponents will have a longer reach. Therefore, you will need to work on techniques for getting into your fighting range without getting nailed. Use footwork techniques to get inside. Use a front kick to guard yourself while getting into range, then use powerful punches to score points. Use a solid back kick to get out of range again and to set up your next attack. Knee strikes will also work well for you, once you can establish your fighting range. Also, use the backfist to score to the high section. Otherwise, opponents will keep the middle section guarded at all times; they'll assume they're in no danger from high kicks.

If you are short but small, you will use some of the same ideas. Work on getting into your fighting range without getting nailed. Use footwork for this, and practice body shifting to avoid attacks. If you're small, use quick, easy scoring techniques such as front kicks and roundhouse kicks once you are in range. Use quick hand techniques such as knife hand and ridge hand strikes to score points, especially to the high section. Work on reaching with the backfist while keeping your midsection guarded.

Tall, big people have some advantages. They have excellent reach and powerful techniques, but they tend to be slower than people of other body types. Practice keeping opponents at a distance. Stop people who want to come inside by using a side kick to the ribs. Follow with a power technique such as a back kick. If your opponent does get inside, use powerful punches and knee strikes to score and to convince him or her to get out of close range.

If you are tall and light, you have the advantage of reach and quickness. With your height, you have an easier time scoring with kicks to the head. However, you must also work to keep people from coming inside. Use roundhouse kicks, especially double kicks, on opponents who try to move inside. Use footwork to keep people from moving in, since it's hard for you to fight at a small person's punching range. Master techniques for moving into your kicking range, such as back stepping and pivot stepping. You can also use jump or step kicks away from your target to establish a better kicking range.

If you're an average-sized person, you have to be adaptable, since your opponents won't always be either shorter than you or taller than you. Work on inside fighting techniques for sparring taller people and work on evasive techniques for avoiding extremely quick or powerful fighters. Remember that many of the greatest Karate practitioners are average-sized people. Their size forces them to become versatile, which in turn helps them to become superior martial artists.

Assessing Your Strengths—Body Type

Short and big: Deliver power blows. Use footwork techniques to get inside. Guard with a front kick while getting into range, and use a solid back kick to get out of range. Use knee strikes in close range. Use the backfist to score to the high section.

Short and small: Use footwork for getting into fighting range and practice body shifting to avoid attacks. Use quick, easy scoring techniques such as front kicks and roundhouse kicks. Quick hand techniques (knife hand and ridge hand strikes), especially to the high section, can be successful.

Tall and big: Keep opponents at a distance. Use a side kick to the ribs to stop people. Use powerful punches and knee strikes to score in close range.

Tall and light: Use high kicks. Use roundhouse kicks, especially double kicks. Use footwork to keep opponents from moving in. Establish a better kicking range with jump or step kicks.

Average-sized: Be adaptable. Work on inside fighting techniques for sparring taller people and work on evasive techniques for avoiding extremely quick or powerful fighters.

Although making an honest assessment of yourself is essential to finding a style of fighting that works best for you, don't use the assessment as an excuse for not mastering difficult techniques or for relying on the same four or five tried-and-true techniques. This makes you an average, one-dimensional fighter. To be a truly superior fighter, you must constantly challenge yourself. Even if you are small and light, you can build more power and mass. If you're already big and powerful, you can develop speed and finesse. See chapter 8 for drills to improve your flexibility, speed, and power.

And don't just stop at one assessment. Every few months, take a few minutes to look at your sparring skills and goals. Where have you improved? Where do you need work? Think of your sparring as a process, a continuing journey, not a destination you will someday arrive at and never have to work at again.

PART III

THE COMPETITIVE EDGE

CHAPTER 7

THE FOCUS

The martial arts inspires an indomitable spirit that one carries as one carries heart and soul.

Sparring seems to be the most physical of all aspects of the martial arts, but it is in fact the one area that requires the most mental discipline.

It takes immense focus and concentration to block out frustrations and distractions that try to creep their way into a sparring match. It takes dedication and perseverance to face challenges that may seem impossible to overcome. And it takes confidence to react quickly and without hesitation in a match. These are just a few of the qualities that must be cultivated through both physical exercise and mental practices such as meditation and visualization. The importance of mental discipline in the martial arts cannot be overlooked, especially in the warrior aspect of martial arts—freestyle sparring.

Characteristics of the Successful Martial Artist

The following are attributes that every martial artist should strive to attain.

Fudoshin

Fudoshin is a Japanese term meaning the ability to remain calm and detached, even when faced with a threat or difficulty. If you can cultivate *fudoshin*, you'll be less concerned about personal harm and risk. Since you won't be fearful or confused, you'll react with a clear and open mind. You'll be able to make good decisions, instead of panicked, poor decisions. *Fudoshin* is one expression of self-control. Fighters who have clear, calm minds will always be more successful than fighters who allow fear and doubt to creep in.

Heijo-Shin

One must have *fudoshin* to develop *heijo-shin,* which is intense focus. A focused mind is essential to preparing for and coping with any great challenge. Some martial artists claim to be able to see when another person has this focus or *heijo-shin.* Such people appear determined. They put forth the greatest effort and work the hardest. *Heijo-shin* filters out all unnecessary stimulation. Developing this quality helps one to remain alert and ready, eliminating fear, surprise, and indecision.

Fighters who have intense focus are not distracted or frustrated when a call goes against them. Fighters with *heijo-shin* are able to block out any distractions and single-mindedly pursue the goal of sparring the opponent perfectly.

Kokoro

Fudoshin and *heijo-shin*—self-control and focus—are necessary for tests of all kinds and are developed through meditation and physical exercise. But these mental attitudes are meaningless without heart or spirit. A martial artist might have great talent, but without *kokoro* (heart or spirit), he or she will ultimately fail. A martial artist without heart is not a true martial artist. A person with *kokoro* will often defeat a person with greater skills but no heart. *Kokoro*, in the end, comes from doing your best and giving your best effort at all times. *Kokoro* is the manifestation of perseverance and indomitable spirit, of trying one's best at all times, no matter the odds. *Kokoro* comes from dedication to the martial arts and from devoted practice.

The Warrior Mindset

Fudoshin: the ability to remain calm and detached, even when faced with a threat or difficulty.

Heijo-Shin: an intensely focused mind, essential to preparing for and coping with any great challenge.

Kokoro: heart or spirit, which comes from doing one's best and giving one's best effort at all times.

Balance

In order to achieve the mental mindset necessary for true martial arts achievement, the fighter must learn balance. Through balance, the fighter learns how to defend as well as attack, to counter as well as initiate, to use a variety of techniques instead of relying on a few. It is balance that, in the end, helps the fighter put the fight into its proper perspective.

Understanding the concept of *yin-yang* (called *um-yang* in Korean) helps a martial artist achieve balance. *Yin-yang* is a description of how the universe works. The universe consists of conflicting yet harmonious elements that depend on each other for their meaning. Day and night, for instance, have no meaning except in their relationship to each other.

Yin symbolizes the destructive elements in the universe, while *yang* symbolizes the creative elements in the universe. These opposites are necessary but incomplete. They must be combined to make a whole. To apply the concept of *yin-yang*, the martial artist must combine the hard and the soft, the passive and the active, to become the best martial artist possible. Understanding *yin-yang* also requires the practice of moderation in all things.

Chi

One of the greatest benefits of martial arts training is the development of *chi*, or inner energy. Everyone has this inner energy, and being able to tap into it is essential for success in all aspects of the martial arts, not just sparring. Being able to focus on and use this inner energy improves your martial arts skills. Martial artists attempt to summon *chi* by shouting. Karate practitioners call this the *kiai;* Taekwondo practitioners call it the *kihop*.

Tapping into *chi* can make you more powerful, focused, and determined. To do this, focus all of your energy on a single target, goal, or task; this requires practice and concentration. By concentrating on perfect execution of physical techniques, you will discipline your mind to focus. Thus, when you practice a side kick that you will use in sparring, you will focus on performing the perfect side kick, without error. You will mentally visualize the perfect side kick, imagine what it feels like, then watch your body as you attempt to create this perfect technique. Nothing should interfere with the physical execution of the technique—not the phone ringing, not your personal doubts about your abilities, nothing. Although your attempt may fall short of perfection, the focus you develop in the attempt is irreplaceable.

When sparring, the martial artist uses *chi* to keep going even when he or she is exhausted and would like to give up. This ability to focus when necessary epitomizes true fighting spirit.

Confidence

Fear, doubt, indecision, and confusion all work to defeat the fighter. But these problems and emotions are the result of the martial artist's own attitude. With dedicated martial arts practice, you can learn to eliminate these destructive beliefs and encourage creative, constructive beliefs and attitudes.

Although sparring obviously requires physical skill, success only comes if you are also mentally prepared. If you are confident as you spar, you will be more likely to react quickly and without hesitation. If you are hesitant or unsure of yourself, you may let opportunities to score pass you by. At first, developing confidence is difficult, since you aren't sure what you're doing. That's why practicing step sparring sequences, timing techniques, and combination drills is so important. These drills help to prepare you for the real thing.

Winning Spirit

The confidence that develops as a result of the focus and the mental and physical skills that sparring requires is necessary to successful martial arts practice.

Other qualities or behaviors are necessary for the fighter to succeed as well. For instance, the ultimate goal of Taekwondo is the development of five qualities that make up good character. These tenets of Taekwondo are courtesy, integrity, perseverance, self-control, and indomitable spirit. These qualities are the essence of true warrior spirit. They, of course, apply outside the training hall or sparring ring as well, but they will certainly be tested when you fight competitively.

Tenets of Taekwondo

- *Courtesy* creates an environment where ego is not supreme and honest self-assessment is possible.
- *Integrity* governs relationships with others, which must always be conducted honestly.
- *Perseverance* prevents giving up, even when a challenge seems impossible to overcome or a goal seems impossible to reach.
- *Self-control* allows restraint, physically and emotionally. It requires using reason and judgment, not fear or anger, to make decisions.
- *Indomitable spirit* is having the right attitude whether winning or losing.

Master Jung's Indomitable Spirit

Several years ago, Jennifer Lawler traveled to Cedar Rapids, Iowa, to watch one of her senior instructors test for fifth dan black belt. While she was there, her instructor's instructor, Grandmaster Woo Jin Jung, took the time to talk with her about the martial arts and how important they are to a world in conflict.

Master Jung shared not only his expertise regarding the skills and strategies necessary for building a powerful sparring arsenal, but also his personal history. His story illustrates the most important features needed for success, not only in the martial arts, but in life, including perseverance, confidence, and heart.

Master Woo Jin Jung was born in a small town in Korea, the youngest of seven children. His family were rice farmers who worked 16 or 18 hours a day, 7 days a week. Master Jung was 9 years old when the Korean War broke out, which caused people in his small town to resort to stealing and other means to prevent starvation. Many did not survive.

When he was about 12 years old, he moved to the city of Pusan, the second largest city in Korea, where his sister lived. His father had always dreamed of him going there to get an education. His brothers and sister made many sacrifices to help pay his tuition for high school.

The city both overawed and intimidated him. People would sometimes harass him, and because he was small for his age, boys would try to beat him up. Soon he heard about someone teaching the martial arts and decided that was what he needed. Each day, he would go to this martial arts school, where he learned the basic techniques of Tang Soo Do, a Korean martial art similar to Karate. He used the money he had for school books to pay his martial arts teacher, and he bought used books instead of new and borrowed them when he could.

The other students at the school treated him like a punching bag at first; he spent most of this time black and blue. But in the end, he was only one of one hundred people who earned a black belt.

Master Jung went on to Seoul to study mechanical engineering in college. This was a dark period, because there were many people going hungry, without jobs. Master Jung went to school part-time, worked in a pipe factory part-time, and taught martial arts part-time. Doing this, he managed to make ends meet and obtain his education.

In 1967 he was conscripted into the army during the Vietnam War. While serving as a soldier, he saw a bomb explode, injuring a U.S. Army repairman. He started to go to the man's aid, but was told to stay back, that there were other bombs. Master Jung realized he was in a minefield, and that the soldier was more concerned about Master Jung's safety than he was about his own injuries. This selfless act convinced Master Jung that someday he wanted to live among Americans.

After finishing his stint in the army, Master Jung was ready to go to the United States. On January 1, 1972, he arrived in California with $35 in his pocket. He worked in a tire shop at first, then took a bus and traveled throughout the country, trying to decide where he would make his home. He liked small cities, so he decided to settle in Cedar Rapids, Iowa. He worked at a gas station before finding the location for his first

Master Jung (on the right) demonstrates his skill and precision by kicking an apple out of his opponent's mouth.

Taekwondo school, which he fixed up himself. In the beginning, he had no car and was always overdrawn at the bank, but he had the American dream of owning his own business.

On the first day his school opened, he had only one student. People didn't know anything about Taekwondo—all they knew was Karate. Since they didn't know much about the martial arts, they would challenge him to fight, thinking that the point of martial arts was to prove they were tougher or stronger than Master Jung. Sometimes these challengers were other martial arts teachers who thought Master Jung might take away their students. One challenger even pulled a knife on him. Through it all, he persevered. Now he has branch schools all over Iowa, and several of his students have opened schools of their own.

Master Jung believes the two most important things people can get from the martial arts are confidence and discipline, as evidenced in his own story. "When people don't practice self-control, they become unhappy," says Master Jung. "They don't take care of themselves and, as a result, become out of shape or gain weight. All of this contributes to physical and emotional distress." Another important benefit is the stress relief that comes from working out. According to Master Jung, "such mental and physical exertion helps people feel recharged and energized and distracts one from everyday worries." Martial arts can make life more exciting, and its lessons last a lifetime.

To Master Jung, teaching is a joy. "It is like being a gardener," he says, "watering flowers, watching them grow, or like being a mother with a child, watching the child take its first steps. I feel truly blessed to have achieved all of my goals and to have watched hundreds of my students grow in the martial arts."

According to traditional Japanese martial arts, five rules should govern the behavior of all athletes, martial artists in particular. These are practices that help the martial artist develop winning spirit and good character. First, one should believe in the philosophy of one's school. If this is not possible, one's loyalty will be misplaced or insincere. Second, one should stay fit regardless of circumstances. This means that even when you are pressed for time or don't have enough money to join a gym, you will do whatever is required to stay in shape. Third, one must be committed to mastering the martial art one has chosen once such a study is undertaken. This means not giving up when training seems too challenging or when other activities attract your interest. It means not trying every martial art style and school in the city for a month or two each, but requires a serious dedication to mastering the chosen art. Fourth, the martial artist must be willing to participate in difficult training. The martial artist must be willing to challenge him or herself, going beyond what is routine or comfortable. He or she must be willing to try new techniques, attempt difficult maneuvers, and continually work harder. Finally, the martial artist must do his or her best in competition.

These elements, called "Resolute in Five Respects," are thought to be fundamental to successful martial arts training. Essentially, one cannot give excuses for not trying hard and doing one's best. This also builds character and makes one a better person.

Resolute in Five Respects

One should believe in the philosophy of one's school.

One should stay fit regardless of circumstances.

One must be committed to mastering the martial art one has chosen.

One must be willing to participate in difficult training.

One must do one's best in competition.

Funakoshi Gichin, the founder of modern Karate, modified these rules slightly and developed five regulations of his own which he expected Karate students to adhere to. These include the commitment to training; the discipline to avoid ego; the necessity to be self-aware; the focus to concern oneself with training, not theory, because studying theory gives one the excuse to quit training; and the responsibility to behave ethically in all areas of life. Being committed to these rules helps Karate practitioners develop a winning attitude and good character.

Karate Founder's Rules

Commitment to training

Discipline to avoid ego

Necessity to be self-aware

Focus to concern oneself with training

Responsibility to behave ethically in all areas of life

Developing a winning attitude is based on having heart, refusing to become discouraged, and giving the best effort possible. With this attitude, the martial artist can achieve beyond his or her expectations and can continue to grow in the martial arts.

Achieving and Maintaining Focus

Now that you know what characteristics are needed for success in sparring, you need to know how they can be developed. In addition to physical discipline and physical effort, you can develop *chi* (inner energy) and focus through a variety of means, including meditation and breathing exercises.

Meditation

Meditation helps develop focus and concentration. Following are several meditation techniques that martial artists use.

Visualization

Visualization is simply a method of imagining how to perform perfectly. After a workout, a martial artist can sit in a relaxed position, eyes closed, and review the session. He or she can consider what went well and why, plus identify areas that need improvement. The martial artist then thinks about how the weaknesses could be overcome. If something about the workout was frustrating or distracting, the martial artist considers why this was so and how the frustration or distraction could be avoided in the future.

Visualization is also used before any test of the martial artist's skills, such as prior to a competition or a sparring match. Again, the martial artist finds a quiet corner, sits in a relaxed position with eyes closed, and imagines how the sparring match will go. He or she will imagine sparring perfectly, avoiding or blocking strikes, delivering attacks that score points, performing without getting a warning or penalty. This type of visualization helps the fighter feel confident going into the match and helps produce a calm and focused mind.

Zazen Meditation

Zazen meditation is a method of meditation in which the martial artist simply controls and then stops all thoughts. The goal is to attain an empty, harmonious mind. Many martial arts, including Taekwondo and Karate, teach this type of meditation. Practicing "empty mind" helps fighters remain calm and detached, leaving them able to cope with the challenges of martial arts practice or competition.

Satori

Satori, or meditation that leads to enlightenment, is attempted in Zen Buddhism. Many Asian religions and philosophies encourage the use of meditation for achieving enlightenment. Some martial artists also attempt this type of meditation for its spiritual benefits.

Breathing Techniques

To help with meditation and to improve focus and concentration, martial artists can use various types of breathing techniques. Most martial artists use at least a simple breathing technique: inhale deeply through the nose, then exhale slowly through the mouth. With this breathing technique, your breath should go deep into your stomach. Your chest *and* your abdomen should both move in and out. Doing this breathing after a workout or at intervals throughout a workout helps your body get enough oxygen. You can increase the intensity and length of your workout by incorporating such breathing techniques.

Focused breathing techniques can be used to control your breathing by deliberately slowing your breath rate, which helps you to recover more quickly from physical exertion. Focused breathing also helps you control everyday stress by calming you down. As you breathe in through the nose and out through the mouth, take a few seconds longer to inhale and exhale between breaths. Gradually extend the length of time between breaths until you are relaxed and can breathe slowly without effort.

To increase lung capacity when you perform focused breathing, extend your arms out to the side while inhaling. Slowly push your hands together while exhaling. Imagine the breath coming into and leaving your lungs as you do this.

Martial artists should be aware of their breathing at all times, especially when performing techniques. Always breathe out while striking with the technique. This helps add focus and power to each technique. Then, inhale when returning to the starting position. Often, when you concentrate on exhaling as you strike, inhaling follows naturally. Don't breathe too rapidly or you'll hyperventilate.

As you become more comfortable with these breathing techniques, you will notice improved endurance during your workouts.

Controlling the Match

Using the mental discipline of focus and perseverance is essential to developing excellent sparring skills. Mental discipline can help you control a sparring match, but it must be linked to physical skills to work. The following tips can help you combine mental and physical skills in order to gain and keep the upper hand in a sparring match.

Don't Let Frustration Take Hold

When sparring, it can be easy to get discouraged or frustrated. Don't let these feelings distract you. Even if your partner is scoring points and you're not, you have to continue fighting confidently. Don't be frustrated or embarrassed by techniques that don't succeed or by counters that are off or by openings that are missed. Learn from these failures instead of being angered or discouraged by them. If your doubts get the better of you, your opponent will have won without scoring a point. A positive attitude is essential to good sparring. Even bad sparring experiences help you learn and grow as a martial artist.

Focus on Yourself

In order to practice more perfectly, worry only about your own sparring. Ask yourself if you're taking advantage of openings that come up or if you're anticipating your partner's techniques. Are you getting faster, stronger, smarter? Don't concern yourself with how you compare to your partner or opponent or other martial artists. Learn to be the best martial artist you can be. The true competition is with yourself. Each sparring match is an opportunity for you to improve.

Don't become anxious about your inability to kick high or to perform a complicated series of techniques. Work on these areas of concern, but remember to play to your strengths. Relax, enjoy the process, and worry only about yourself, not what the other fighter is doing.

Stay in the Game

A fighter that can rattle his or her opponent has won half the battle. That's why some fighters talk trash. If they can make opponents mad, their opponents will no longer be in the game. By getting their opponents to focus on them instead of on sparring, they make them more vulnerable to defeat. Such maneuvers might be called "psyching the opponent out" or "getting the opponent out of their game."

While this may seem like a cheap way to defeat an opponent (it might even seem like cheating), enough fighters do it that you have to be aware of it and not allow it to affect you. A good referee or ring judge will usually put a stop to deliberate provocation, but some who lack experience won't. This means you'll have to focus harder not to let your opponent get you out of your game.

The fighter who controls the energy and momentum of a match has a good chance of winning it. This is why some fighters use any method they can think of to distract the opponent. But just because such distractions help fighters win matches doesn't mean you should resort to unsportsmanlike conduct. Instead, control the match by sparring with skill and confidence.

Some fighters use different tactics to try to psych out their opponents. A sparring match starts when the judge or instructor says "go," and the two contestants signal their intention to fight by giving a *kihop* or *kiai*. Some fighters will shout and kick at the same time, thinking the split second difference will give them a valuable edge. In fact, many fighters think this is a great tactic. Others call it cheating (you're supposed to wait until *after* you *kihop* or *kiai* to begin sparring). If you are matched with an opponent who uses this tactic, you cannot hope to reason with him or her. You must simply anticipate what the fighter is going to do and then avoid the kick. How? Watch plenty of sparring matches to learn the tricks that fighters use, and then get ready for them.

One way to anticipate moves is to always look your opponent in the eye as you spar. This is basic but hard to remember. Don't watch your partner's arms and legs to see what kicks or punches might be coming your way. Learn to respond instinctively as you sense a strike coming. Keeping your eyes up sends a message of confidence and also helps you from getting distracted and falling for feints and other techniques that might cause you to lower your guard.

Another psych-out tactic is to target illegal areas just to arouse one's opponent. In Taekwondo, for example, all techniques must be above the opponent's waist. Most fighters try to hit their opponents in target areas only. If they accidentally make contact to a nontarget area, they will apologize. Some fighters, on the other hand, think a nontarget area is simply an area that doesn't count toward a point total. Some will routinely strike to nontarget areas simply to see what the response will be. They know that such a strike doesn't count as a point, but they don't see that trying to make contact to a nontarget area is wrong. For example, a fighter might continually kick to your hip, even though he won't score any points for it, just to get you frustrated or angry so you won't spar as well. Of course, repeated strikes to a nontarget area can result in a penalty, but if you let it get to you, your opponent will have won the match anyway. Don't allow such tactics to disturb, discourage, or frustrate you. Of course, if your opponent is acting dangerously, you should withdraw from the match.

Remember, the true competition is against yourself. Focus on what you do. Did you counter that strike, or was your timing off? Did you block when you could have countered? Did you keep pushing your opponent back, or did you quit pursuing once you executed two techniques in a row? By cultivating the right mental attitude, you will be able to compete with calm assurance and feel confident about yourself and your abilities, win or lose.

CHAPTER 8

THE FITNESS

The body is the machine that carries one's dreams. A fit machine can make dreams come true.

Martial artists should vary their routines depending on whether or not they're gearing up for competition. Start intensive training about three months before a tournament. Step it up about a month before so that you hit your peak at tournament time. Plan to enter a backup tournament at the same time so that if you don't perform as well as you'd like, you can make it up.

If you plan to follow the tournament season, you should take a slightly different approach. The tournament season can last weeks or months. During this period, you should keep your training moderately intense. Don't train with serious intensity the entire time or you'll risk injury and burnout. Plan the intense training for special tournaments, such as national or international competition, and keep your training at a slightly modified intensity for the local and regional events you use for tune-ups.

Even in the off-season, you should continue practicing your sparring and other aspects of the martial arts at least three or four times per week. This way, you will stay in good condition and can reach your peak during competition times.

In order to maintain the body conditioning necessary to spar well, you'll need to follow some basic guidelines. First, you should always warm up and stretch before any workout. Then, you should add strength, flexibility, and speed drills to your basic martial arts workout for optimum sparring performance.

Warm-Up and Stretching

Before you begin any exercise routine, you need to warm up and stretch. Working out with cold muscles significantly increases the risk of strains, sprains, and tears, not to mention tendinitis and bursitis. Keep this part of the program simple unless you're prone to injuries, in which case you should increase the amount of time you spend stretching.

Although stretching is important, it should never be done with cold muscles either. Begin every workout with a few minutes of aerobic activity. Hop on the treadmill or the bike for a few minutes, starting slowly and then increasing the speed or difficulty. Walk briskly, jump rope, or climb the stairs a few times if you don't have access to aerobic equipment. Aim for about five minutes of warm-up activity. When you break a light sweat, you're ready to stretch.

Stretching helps your muscles prepare for a physical workout. Use care when stretching to avoid injury. Don't bounce or jerk. Move smoothly to the stretch position and hold the stretch for about 10 seconds. Then slowly release and return to your starting position.

The several stretches described here are also useful in martial arts training because they prepare the muscles for kicking and punching. Feel free to add stretches as needed. As you stretch, think of moving from the top of your body down. This way, you won't forget to warm up your hips or back because you got distracted.

NECK STRETCH

Stretch your neck in each of the four directions. Begin by tucking your chin toward your chest. Hold this position for 10 seconds. Then, tilt your head to the left. Hold this position for 10 seconds. Next, hold your head to the right, holding the position for 10 seconds. Finally, look up toward the ceiling, feeling the back of your head touch your back. Hold for 10 seconds.

SHOULDER STRETCH

Extend your arm parallel to the floor. Sweep it across your chest. You should feel the stretch in the back of your shoulder/upper arm. Use your other hand to hold for a better stretch. Hold the stretch for 10 seconds. Then relax and, keeping the arm parallel to the ground, reach to the back. Don't twist at the waist. Hold for 10 seconds. Relax and repeat three or four times for each shoulder.

WRIST STRETCH

To loosen your wrist and hand, extend your arm slightly in front of your body. Keeping your palm open, pull your fingers back. Hold for 10 seconds. Then press your fingers down. Hold for 10 seconds. Repeat five times for each hand.

BACK STRETCH

Sit on the floor with your legs crossed. Gently bend your body toward the floor. Try to touch your chin to your legs. If you feel mild discomfort (or pain), relax the stretch. Don't bounce. Hold for 10 seconds, relax, and repeat. To get a better stretch, reach your arms in front of you, then bend them at the elbows, trying to touch the floor.

HIP FLEXOR STRETCH

The flexor muscle is on top of the hip, running from the lower abdomen to the thigh. This muscle is easily strained, especially in fighters, so don't neglect it. To stretch this muscle, kneel on the floor. Keeping your upper body straight, slowly roll your hip forward. Feel the stretch on the top of your hip and thigh. If you need to support yourself, do so by placing your hands on the floor. Hold the forward position for about 10 seconds, then relax and repeat.

GROIN STRETCH

Sit on the floor, legs extended. Slide your feet toward you, bending your knees until the soles of your feet are touching. Your knees should be out to the side. Hold the position for 10 seconds. For a better stretch, lean forward, trying to touch your forehead to your feet. Hold this position for 10 seconds. Relax and repeat.

OPEN STRETCH

Sit with your legs spread in a V-shape as far apart as possible. Bending at the waist, lean toward your left leg. Try to touch the bottom of your left foot with your hands. Keep your back straight and don't bend your knee. Hold the position for 10 seconds, then relax and stretch again. Repeat five times on both sides. For an additional stretch, bend at the waist and lean forward between your legs. Try to stretch forward so that your chest rests on the ground. Hold this position for 10 seconds, then relax and repeat five times.

BICYCLE STRETCH

To stretch hip and back muscles, perform this stretch. Lie on your back (using a mat for comfort and support). Slide your hands under the small of your back for additional support if needed. Lift your legs in the air and move them in a circular motion, as if you were riding a bike. "Bicycle" for 20 seconds, then reverse direction and "bicycle" in the opposite direction for 20 seconds.

HAMSTRING STRETCH

Lie on your back. Place your hands or a rolled-up towel under the small of your back for support. Lift your leg up and extend it at a 90-degree angle to the floor. Move your leg toward your chest. Keep your leg straight (don't bend your knee), and try to touch your knee to your shoulder. You can use your hands to pull your leg toward you. If you don't have enough flexibility for this, you can use a towel like a sling around your calf and pull on the ends of the towel to bring your leg forward. Be certain not to overdo it, and don't bounce. When your leg is at its full stretch, hold for 10 seconds, then relax and repeat. Slowly lower your leg to the floor and stretch the other leg.

QUADRICEPS STRETCH

Put one hand on a wall for support. Extend your leg out behind you and bend your knee. With your free hand, reach behind and pull your foot toward your buttocks. Lift your leg so that your quadriceps (front of the thigh) faces the floor. Hold this position for 10 seconds. Repeat five times on each leg.

CALF RAISES

Use a wall for support if necessary. Standing straight, lift your heels off the ground until you are standing on your toes. Hold this stretch for 10 seconds. Lower your heels to the ground and rock back until your toes are off the ground. Hold this stretch for 10 seconds. Then repeat five times.

STANCE STRETCHES

Stance stretches work well to stretch several main muscle groups while improving your martial arts techniques at the same time. Position yourself in any of the stances that you have been taught. Then lower your stance until you feel the stretch. Hold for about 10 seconds, relax, and repeat.

Some of the most common stance stretches are the horse stance, the front stance, and the back stance. These stance stretches also build up leg strength. Some martial artists challenge themselves by holding deep stances for increasingly longer periods of time.

Avoid deep stance stretches if you have knee problems.

Strength Training

Once you've stretched, you'll want to devote part of your workout to strength, speed, and flexibility drills.

Lifting Weights

To build strength, many martial artists rely on weightlifting. You can do this as part of your martial arts workout or as a separate workout.

Martial artists who lift weights need to avoid bulking up too much or they'll lose speed and flexibility. Most martial artists are satisfied with weight training two or three times a week, doing a complete body workout during these sessions. If you want to incorporate weight training into your workout, keep this rule of thumb in mind: lift enough weight to exhaust your muscles after 8 to 10 repetitions. Using lighter weights and more repetitions than this won't give most martial artists the power they're looking for. Doing fewer repetitions with more weight tends to add more muscle bulk than most martial artists find desirable. So stick with 8 to 10 repetitions for the best results.

Hitting the main muscle groups and concentrating on the arms and legs will enhance martial arts performance. Free weights or machine weights can be used. Although there are pros and cons to each, for the most part it makes sense to simply use what's available and easiest to use. If you're lifting to build strength for martial arts techniques, include these lifts:

- Chest press/bench press
- Butterfly press/bench fly
- Lateral pull-down
- Lateral raise
- Biceps curl
- Triceps extension

- Squat/leg press
- Hamstring curl
- Leg extension

Plan Your Workouts

Plan your lifts so that you use the major muscle groups first before moving on to the smaller muscle groups. For example, you should perform the leg press, which works the thighs, hips, and calves, before you perform a hamstring curl, which works just the hamstring. The chest press should be performed before the triceps extension. This keeps you from exhausting the smaller muscles before you get a chance to target them.

Practice Proper Form

How you perform these lifts depends on whether you're using barbells, dumbbells, or machine weights. Any weightlifting guide will help you learn correct form. Try *Muscle Mechanics* by Everett Aaberg (Human Kinetics, 1998) or *Weight Training for Martial Artists* by Jennifer Lawler (Turtle Press, 1998). If you belong to a gym, the fitness manager will show you how to execute the lifts using proper technique.

The correct form is slightly different for each lift, but some general rules always apply:

- Always lift smoothly and evenly. Don't lift too quickly because that can cause injury. Lifting and lowering a weight should take a total of eight to ten seconds—four or five seconds to lift and four or five seconds to lower.
- Don't lock your joints out when you lift. This is a sure way to injure your joints.
- Be sure to breathe as you lift, exhaling during the exertion.

If you're using a machine, you should have enough control so that the weight plates don't bang together as you set them down. If you can't control the weight plates, go with a lighter weight. Adjust the seat height and distance before using a weight machine. Be certain you understand how to work the machine before you use it.

If you're using free weights, know the proper form for each exercise. Never lift weights by bending from your waist; always bend your knees to lift. Be careful to tighten collars on weight plates so that they don't come loose. Make sure you use a spotter whenever you are working in a position where a dropped weight could cause physical harm. Also, use a spotter when you try to lift more weight than usual, when trying out a new exercise, and when trying more reps than usual.

Strength Training Without Equipment

If you don't have access to weight equipment, you can build strength by using your own body weight as resistance. Crunches, push-ups, and pull-ups or chin-ups are the best ways you can increase strength without equipment (aside from a pull-up bar). In fact, these exercises can actually be more effective on the target areas than weight training and are hard to duplicate in the weight room. Doing crunches will tone your abdominal muscles more effectively than using an ab machine at the gym will. For this reason it is a good idea to add a series of crunches and push-ups to every lifting session to increase your power and conditioning. Do these right after your stretches so that you don't forget.

CRUNCHES

Crunches work your abdominal muscles. (Sit-ups are not recommended because of the stress they put on your back and neck.)

To perform a basic crunch, lie on the floor with your knees bent and your feet flat on the floor. Put your hands behind your ears. Don't put your hands under your neck and don't lace your fingers together. This puts too much strain on your neck.

Using your abdominal muscles, roll forward so that your shoulders lift off the ground. Exhale as you do so. Moving slowly and deliberately, return to your starting position. Inhale as you go. Move slowly and smoothly to avoid using momentum instead of muscles to do the work. Repeat the crunch 15 times.

Following are a number of variations you can use (avoid these if you have back problems):

1. Twist to the right as you crunch by leading with your left shoulder. Try to touch your left elbow to your right knee. Then twist to the left by leading with your right shoulder. Try to touch your right elbow to your left knee. This type of crunch works your oblique abdominal muscles, which are otherwise hard to tone.

2. Cross one leg over the other so that the ankle of one leg rests on the thigh of the other. Keep the foot of the supporting leg flat on the floor. Perform a set of crunches, then switch legs and perform another set of crunches.

3. Lift both legs into the air. Cross one leg over the other. Keeping both legs in the air, perform a set of crunches. Then switch legs.

4. Extend your legs and lift them in the air at a 90-degree angle to the floor. Then perform a set of crunches. Next, lower your legs about six inches and perform a set of crunches. Continue lowering your legs in six-inch increments, performing a set of crunches at each stage.

BOXER SIT-UPS

Boxer sit-ups require a partner. Lie on your back, head slightly between the feet of your partner, who should be standing. Grasp your partner's ankles for support. Raise your legs 90 degrees. Have your partner push your legs down forcefully. Don't let them touch the ground. Lift your legs back up and have your partner push them down again. Work as quickly as possible. Repeat 15 times.

As a variation, have your partner push your legs to the right or the left instead of straight down.

ROPE-UPS

Lie on your back and lift your legs up 90 degrees. Imagine that a rope extends from the ceiling to your legs. Keep your legs on this imaginary line as you roll your hips off the ground. Imagine that you are trying to touch the ceiling with your feet. Move slowly and smoothly through the exercise without pausing. Repeat 15 times.

PUSH-UPS

To perform a basic push-up, lie flat on the floor, palms on the floor directly under your shoulders. Keep your abdomen tight and your back and shoulders straight. Push straight up. Rest your knees on the floor if necessary. Repeat 15 times.

Other variations work different muscle groups. These are done by changing the placement of your hands:

1. Spread your hands so they are extended two shoulder widths apart to work your shoulder muscles.

2. Bring your hands in close under your sternum to work your triceps.

3. Make your hands into fists and rest your weight on the first two knuckles (the punching knuckles) of each hand. This strengthens the wrists and forearms.

PULL-UPS

If a pull-up bar (sometimes called a chin-up bar) is available, work on pull-ups. If necessary, use a spotter (the spotter should grasp your hips and help you lift yourself up). Grip the bar with hands about shoulder-width apart and pull straight up. Your goal should be to perform five or more without a spotter's help.

Variations work different muscle groups. These can be done by changing your grip on the bar. You can widen your grip (which works the back and triceps) or use a backward grip (which works the biceps).

Strength Training Using Martial Arts Techniques

Practicing kicks and punches full power is a time-tested way to increase strength. You'll need a heavy bag (or a strong partner with a kicking target) to do this. Your goal should be to knock the heavy bag back with every technique. Practice your techniques in a continuous two-minute round to improve your endurance for sparring. Avoid using axe kicks, hooking kicks, and spinning kicks at full power because the impact can injure the knee. Use side kicks, roundhouse kicks, and reverse (back) kicks. You can also use almost any hand, knee, or elbow strike.

If you don't have access to a heavy bag or a cooperative partner, you can build strength through practicing martial arts techniques by slow motion kicking. This drill is worth doing even if you do have a partner and a heavy bag.

Begin by practicing your techniques slowly in front of a mirror. Tense your muscles throughout the movement and try to perform the technique as perfectly as possible. Although you can practice hand techniques in slow motion, the real strength building comes when you practice kicks slowly. Use this time to improve your techniques. For instance, when you are performing slow motion side kicks, look at your chamber. Is it high? Is it tight? Is your foot in the correct position? Is your body straight? As you get the hang of kicking slowly (it requires practice), slow down your kicks even more until they look as if they're being done in slow motion. Gradually increase the amount of time it takes for you to do each kick. Your goal should be to spend an entire 60 seconds on one technique. Remember to practice using both legs even if you favor one leg over the other. Balance is essential to the martial artist.

Traditional Strength Training Methods

Traditional strength training methods have been used by martial artists for centuries—before weight machines were invented and gyms were built on every corner. If you do decide to practice a traditional strength training method, use care to prevent injury.

Striking Post: In Korean, the *dalyeun-ju*. In Japanese, the *makiwara* board. A thick piece of lumber with padding attached to it, which the martial artist strikes with punches or other hand techniques.

Mook Jong: Wooden dummy used in Wing Chun and other martial arts to increase striking and trapping skills. Striking the dummy conditions the hands and arms and can improve speed.

Kan Shu: Container filled with abrasive material, such as sand or even gravel. The martial artist repeatedly thrusts his or her hands into this pail. Progressively harder materials are used as the hands grow tougher. This conditions the hands and strengthens hand and arm muscles.

Kame: Containers filled with heavy materials, such as stones. They are lifted and carried to increase grip strength and arm strength.

Chashi or *Sashi:* Chinese training device made from a block of stone. A handle is attached, making the *chashi* resemble a barbell or a dumbbell. The martial artist performs forms *(kata or hyung)* while carrying the device.

Flexibility Training

To balance the work they do on strength and power, martial artists need to incorporate flexibility training into their workouts. Flexibility training also helps the fighter spar better. Higher kicks and faster techniques result from increased flexibility.

One way to increase flexibility is simply to do more stretches. These can be incorporated into daily life as well as being used in the workout. For example, watch television while performing an open stretch. Do shoulder stretches at your desk at work. By thinking of ways to do stretches during your everyday routine, you can significantly increase your flexibility without adding a lot of time to your workout session.

In addition, the following drills will improve flexibility:

HAMSTRING LIFT

Stand with your back against a wall for support. Perform a front kick, keeping your leg extended. Hold the leg in the extended position for 15 seconds. Then relax and repeat with the other leg. Kick and hold your leg higher with each attempt. Do five lifts with each leg. For a better stretch, have a partner hold your extended leg and push up until you feel the stretch. Hold the position while your partner slowly releases your leg. Don't let your leg drop. Count to 15, then lower your leg and repeat with the other leg.

GROIN LIFT

Stand with your side against the wall for support. Perform a side kick, keeping your leg extended. Hold the leg in the extended position for 15 seconds. Relax and repeat with the other leg. Kick and hold your leg higher with each attempt. Do five lifts with each leg. For a better stretch, have a partner hold your extended leg and push up until you feel the stretch. Hold the position while your partner slowly releases your leg. Don't let your leg drop. Count to 15, then lower your leg and repeat with the other leg.

CHAMBERING DRILL

Stack targets or cushions on the floor or a low bench. Practice chambering your kick high enough to kick over the top of the cushions without knocking them over. Remember to rechamber the kick before returning to the starting position. Practice each of the kicks you know, adding cushions or targets as your skill and flexibility increase.

Speed Training

Speed training will improve your sparring. If you can respond to an opening the moment you see it, you'll be more successful as a fighter. If your techniques are performed quickly, your opponent will have difficulty blocking them, avoiding them, and countering them.

The games you played as a kid are great for building speed. Remember hopscotch? It, plus jump rope and other physical games, can build speed considerably. If you're not inclined to jump rope, or you've forgotten the rules to hopscotch, the following are basic speed exercises that will help you improve your agility and quickness.

FROG JUMPS

Squat on the floor. Use your hands for balance, but don't let them touch the ground. Leap-frog your way across the room as quickly as possible. Keep up continual leap-frogging for 30 seconds, adding on 5 seconds at a time. Your goal is to do 60 frog jumps in 60 seconds.

JUMPING DRILL

Stack cushions or targets on the floor. (Don't try this drill with hard materials such as chairs or benches; the risk of injury is too great.) Start with a stack about eight inches high. Jump from one side of the stack to the other as quickly as you can without stopping or knocking the cushions over. Jump at least 10 times before pausing. Stack the cushions higher as you improve. Your goal is to stack the cushions as high as your knees and complete 20 jumps in 30 seconds.

SWEEPING DRILL

You'll need a partner for this drill. Use a blocking target if possible. If a blocking target is not available, any long, flexible object will do. Your partner should sweep at your feet. Jump up to avoid hitting the target. Your partner should sweep back and forth quickly, without allowing pauses between jumps. As you improve, have your partner increase the height at which he or she sweeps. Your goal is to jump over a knee-high target 30 times in 30 seconds.

PUNCHING DRILL

This drill can be done with or without a partner. If you don't have a partner, use a heavy bag. If you do have a partner, have him or her hold a target. Position yourself so that at full extension your arm just touches the target. Strike to the target using a hand technique, such as a punch, moving as quickly as possible. Return your hand to the chamber position twice as fast as you punch out with it. Use good technique. You should be able to strike about 60 times per half-minute. Build up from there. Remember to train both sides equally.

For a variation, alternate punches. Perform a straight punch, then a reverse punch, then a straight punch.

Speed in sparring is also a matter of response time. In order to improve your ability to spot an opening and then strike to it, work on these response time drills:

HAND RESPONSE TIME DRILL

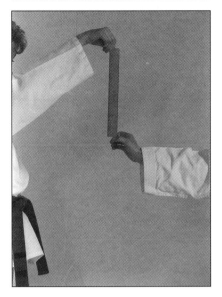

Work with a partner. Extend your arm and have your partner place the "zero" end of a ruler between your thumb and forefinger. (Your partner should hold the ruler so that it is perpendicular to the floor.) The end of the ruler should barely rest between your fingers. Keep your thumb and forefinger about an inch apart. Have your partner let go of the ruler at random. Pinch it between your fingers as quickly as possible. Don't move your hand up or down; simply close your finger and thumb together. Record the measurement at which you caught the ruler (for example, 3 1/4 inches or about 8 1/4 centimeters). Practice until you can catch the ruler in the first few inches or centimeters.

KICK RESPONSE TIME DRILL

Work with a partner. Assume a fighting stance and have your partner hold a target (any kind) in front of you. Have your partner say "go" at random intervals. As soon as you hear the word, kick to the target using any technique. Practice until you can hit the target almost immediately after hearing the signal.

KICK RESPONSE TIME VARIATION

Work with a partner. Assume a fighting stance and have your partner hold a sheet of paper about shoulder high, a few feet away (it should be in kicking range). Your partner should let go of the paper at random. Strike the paper with any kicking technique before it touches the ground or floats out of range. Since the paper doesn't fall directly to the ground, it requires you to make adjustments in your kick to strike it.

The conditioning drills and exercises in this chapter will help you get into and maintain fighting shape. By varying your conditioning routine, you can stay in top form whether you're training for competition or not. By adding speed, strength, and flexibility to your workout, you'll gain a competitive edge over other fighters.

CHAPTER 9
THE TIMING

A walk through the jungle after the lion has eaten is beautiful. A walk through the jungle when the lion is hungry is short. Timing is everything.

In sparring, timing is crucial. You need to see an opening and strike immediately. But often, by the time a fighter sees an opening and reacts, the opening is gone. Timing drills help you anticipate openings and respond with the right technique.

Each fighting technique has inherent strengths and weaknesses. Learning what the weaknesses are and exploiting them is the point of timing techniques. For example, the roundhouse kick is a good kick to use to reach someone's head. Its weakness is that it can leave your chest open. Therefore, if your partner performs a roundhouse kick, and you've been practicing your timing techniques, you will know to immediately throw a punch to your partner's chest, which is open and unblocked.

The following timing technique drills will help you hone these skills. Although these drills require a partner, you can practice them on a heavy bag or in front of a mirror. To get a true feel for the techniques, however, you will need to work with a partner.

Basic Timing Drills

To understand the meaning of timing and how you can use it in sparring, start with basic timing drills. Once you have mastered them, build on them by adding more difficult timing techniques.

Blocks

As you begin freestyle sparring, you will be concerned with blocking your opponent's techniques. Blocking a technique allows you to avoid the attack and keeps your opponent from scoring on you. You can then move in with an attack of your own. Although several blocking drills follow, you can also devise your own.

PUNCH BLOCK

Both partners should assume fighting stances. Have your partner punch to your middle section with his or her forward hand. Block this punch with your forward hand using any block you choose. Practice until you are comfortable with actually knocking your partner's hand out of the way. Once you are, add a new element: block with your forward hand, then punch to your partner's middle section with your back hand. Karate practitioners can punch to the head. Add another punch with your forward hand. *Kihop* or *kiai* to show that you have finished. Return to your original stance.

SIDE KICK BLOCK

Both partners should assume fighting stances with chests facing in the same direction. Have your partner perform a side kick. Perform a low or downward block to sweep your partner's leg out of the way. Your low block should be done with your forward hand, and you should block down over your forward leg. Once you are comfortable with this block, add a counterattack of your own. Sweep your partner's leg out of the way, trying to create an unguarded opening to the chest. If you block quickly and with confidence, you can often cause your partner to lower his or her guard. Step forward with your back leg and punch with your back hand. Karate practitioners can punch to the head; Taekwondo practitioners must keep this punch to the middle section. *Kihop* or *kiai* to show that you are done. Return to your original stance.

Practice this timing technique until you move quickly and smoothly, starting the block and punch as soon as you see the side kick coming. By identifying the side kick before it is extended, you will learn to anticipate openings and start your counterattack before your opponent has even finished striking.

FRONT KICK BLOCK

You can use the same technique as the side kick block to block a front kick. In this case, be sure to block directly downward to move the kick out of the way. Again, follow up with a counterattack such as a reverse punch. Karate practitioners can punch to the head; Taekwondo practitioners must punch to the middle section.

REVERSE KICK BLOCK

Both partners should assume fighting stances with chests facing in opposite directions. Have your partner perform a reverse kick. Perform a low block with your forward arm, pushing or sweeping the reverse kick aside. Be sure to push the kick in the same direction your partner is already rotating to use your partner's own momentum against him or her. *Kihop* or *kiai* to show that you are finished. Return to your original stance.

Once you are comfortable blocking the reverse kick, add a punch by stepping in with your back leg and punching to the middle section with your back hand. Karate practitioners can punch high.

Practice countering other kicks, too, such as the roundhouse kick.

Punches and Hand Strikes

As you grow more proficient with your timing techniques, you will no longer need to block the kicks and punches before counterattacking. You will simply step, weave, or duck out of the way using footwork or body shifting and then counter. The best way to try this is to modify the timing techniques you have already been doing. Although several drills follow, you can devise your own.

PUNCHING AGAINST A SIDE KICK

Both partners should assume fighting stances with chests facing the same way. Have your partner perform a side kick with his or her forward leg. Instead of blocking the kick, step to the side (so that you are on the same side as your partner's chest). Then, step forward and punch to the middle section. *Kihop* or *kiai* to show that you are finished. Return to your original stance. Karate practitioners can use backfists, ridge hands, or knife hand strikes. They can also strike to the head.

PUNCHING AGAINST A REVERSE KICK

Both partners should assume fighting stances with chests facing in opposite directions. Have your partner perform a reverse kick. Instead of blocking the kick, avoid it by using backward stepping: step back with your back foot, then slide your front foot back (photo a). You will end in the same stance, facing in the same direction. You will simply have moved out of kicking range. Then step forward

with your back leg and punch to the middle section with your back hand (photo b). Karate practitioners can use any hand technique and can strike to the head. *Kihop* or *kiai* to show that you are finished. Return to the original stance.

Practice countering other kicks this way, such as the roundhouse kick.

Kicks

As you master blocking and punching timing techniques, you will learn the strengths and weaknesses of different hand techniques and kicks. Knowing the weaknesses of a given technique helps you counter it. It also helps you improve your techniques so that your weaknesses are harder to exploit. For example, when your partner performs a reverse kick and you exploit the weakness (your partner's chest is unguarded and you can easily punch to it), you will realize that when you perform a reverse kick, you should be careful to guard your chest. This way, even if your opponent tries to counter with a punch, you will be ready to block it.

Blocking and punching drills set the stage for kicking drills. Countering kicks with kicks is a more difficult method of timing, but it is also more successful, since you don't have to worry about blocking the technique and you don't have to move into punching or hand striking range. Using a kick to counter a kick is also faster than using a block or moving into punching range and delivering a hand strike. Thus, your counterattack can be performed before your opponent has even finished striking.

Although several drills follow, you can devise your own using techniques of your preference.

REVERSE KICK AGAINST A SIDE KICK

With a partner, assume fighting stances with chests facing in opposite directions. Have your partner perform a side kick using the front leg (photo a, page 140). As soon as you see your partner chamber the kick, immediately turn and perform a reverse kick, striking to your partner's middle section (photo b, page 140). Don't block the side kick and then perform your technique. Simply by turning to do the reverse kick, you will avoid the side kick and you will take advantage of the opening that your partner's side kick has created. *Kihop* or *kiai* to show that you are finished. Return to your original stance.

Once you're comfortable with the timing, add a reverse punch after the reverse kick. Karate practitioners can target the head with this punch.

Reverse kick against a side kick.

REVERSE KICK AGAINST A REVERSE KICK

With a partner, assume fighting stances with chests facing in opposite directions. Have your partner perform a reverse kick (photo a). As soon as you see your

partner chamber the kick, perform a reverse kick of your own (photo b). Don't block your partner's reverse kick first. By turning to do the reverse kick, you will avoid your partner's reverse kick and can take advantage of the opening that will follow. *Kihop* or *kiai* to show that you are finished. Return to your original stance.

Once you're comfortable with the timing, add a reverse punch.

REVERSE KICK AGAINST A ROUNDHOUSE KICK

With a partner, assume fighting stances with chests facing in opposite directions. Have your partner perform a back leg roundhouse kick (photo a). As soon as your partner chambers the kick, perform a reverse kick (photo b). Don't block the roundhouse kick. By turning to do the reverse kick, you will avoid your partner's kick and can take advantage of the opening that will follow. *Kihop* or *kiai* to show that you are finished. Return to your original stance.

SPINNING WHEEL KICK AGAINST A SPINNING WHEEL KICK

Although only Taekwondo competitors do spinning wheel kicks in competition, Karate practitioners can improve their timing by practicing this sequence as well.

With a partner, assume fighting stances with chests facing in opposite directions. Have your partner perform a spinning wheel kick. As soon as you see your partner begin the spinning wheel kick, perform a spinning wheel kick of your own. Don't block your partner's kick. By doing your own spinning wheel kick, you will avoid your partner's kick and can take advantage of the opening that will follow. *Kihop* or *kiai* to show that you are finished. Return to your original stance.

Advanced Timing Drills

Once you've become comfortable with the previous timing drills, you can move on to more difficult drills. The best way to do this is to have both partners work on timing at the same time. For example, suppose your partner does a reverse kick. You know that a good timing technique to counter that kick is a reverse kick, so you perform a reverse kick. But then your partner sees your reverse kick coming and blocks it, following with a punch to your middle section. By combining several different drills, you and your partner can increase your skills and develop good freestyle sparring habits. Try putting together the different drills listed earlier and add your own variations as you become more skilled.

EXTENDED TIMING DRILL

With a partner, assume fighting stances. Partner A performs a roundhouse kick. Partner B counters with a reverse kick. Partner A counters with a reverse punch. Partner B counters with a crescent kick (Taekwondo competitors can perform an axe kick).

Keep the techniques and counters coming smoothly and quickly. Don't pause between techniques. This timing drill can also be used when Partner A leads off with a side kick or a reverse kick.

GEAR KICKING

This timing technique requires skill and confidence. Both partners perform the same kicks, but they perform them repeatedly. The partners should move like the gears of a clock. Partner A performs a reverse kick. Partner B counters with a reverse kick. Partner A responds with another reverse kick. This continues until either partner makes a mistake. The goal is to perform as many successive kicks as you can without mistakes.

Gear kicking should flow smoothly without any stops or pauses. You should finish one technique and immediately begin the next.

The spinning wheel kick can also be used for gear kicking.

Combination Drills

Martial artists frequently fall into a predictable routine when they spar. One partner will do a side kick. The other partner will do a reverse kick. The first partner will do a front kick. The other partner will do a punch. The fighters are only doing one or two techniques at a time. But the more techniques you can perform in a series, the more likely you will be to create an opening, lower your opponent's guard, and distract or overwhelm him or her. To break a predictable rhythm, practice combination drills.

Combination drills make you perform a series of more than one or two techniques in a row. These drills help you understand how techniques flow and how to follow one technique with another. For example, if you perform a roundhouse kick and set your leg down so that you are in a modified horse stance position, you are at the perfect starting point to do a reverse kick. Therefore, a roundhouse kick–reverse kick combination can flow easily without wasted effort. Or perhaps you are working on your spinning wheel kick. Because you still have some momentum helping you to rotate after your kick, you can add a reverse kick. A spinning wheel–reverse kick combination is a good one. However, if you perform a front kick and then try to follow it with a spinning wheel kick, you won't have as much success. This is because such a combination does not flow smoothly. The following combination drills will help you to understand the flow of techniques.

BASIC COMBINATION DRILL

For the basic combination drill, face your partner. Both of you should be in fighting stances. As you *kihop* or *kiai*, your partner moves backward so that you don't hit him or her with any of your techniques. Perform two techniques of any kind and *kihop* or *kiai* to signal that you are finished. Then your partner should perform two techniques as you move backward. Then, perform three techniques of any kind, adding a *kihop* or *kiai* when you are finished. Have your partner do the same. Continue adding one technique to each series until you are doing five or six techniques in a row. When it is your turn to perform combinations, choose different techniques each time and put them in a different order. You and your partner can also discuss which techniques seemed to work well together and which did not.

As you put your combinations together, remember to start with kicking techniques. Continue and end with punches and hand strikes. This is because when you spar, you will usually start in kicking range and then move into punching range. It makes sense to practice your techniques in the same way.

ADVANCED COMBINATION DRILLS

As you become better at combination drills, increase your speed. Your goal is to perform your techniques quickly, as if you were freestyle sparring. To increase your speed, chase your partner. Move quickly enough to land a technique even though your partner is moving away. Wear sparring equipment for this drill.

As a variation, have your partner call out a number from two to eight (more, if you wish) before you begin your series of techniques. This is the number of techniques you must do in a row. Do the same for your partner. Call out a different number each time. By varying the number of techniques you do each time, you are less likely to fall into a predictable rhythm as you spar.

COMBINATION DRILLS WITHOUT A PARTNER

If you don't have a partner, you can practice combination drills yourself. Simply imagine that you are attacking an opponent and perform a series of different techniques each time. Although it is certainly more realistic to practice these drills with a partner, the lack of one should not keep you from practicing. Sparring a heavy bag also helps you string techniques together in a smooth attack sequence.

Mental discipline, physical readiness, and excellent technique—these are meaningless if you don't have timing. Timing is the crucial element in sparring, the key to making everything work together for sensational performance. By working on timing techniques, you'll learn how to spot openings, take advantage of your opponent's fighting style, anticipate techniques, and fight like a warrior.

CHAPTER 10
THE ARSENAL

The strongest weapon in your arsenal is your mind. It is most difficult to defeat the calm, humble person.

Once you've mastered the basics of sparring, it's time to move up a notch. All fighters, even advanced ones, need to keep working on existing skills and mastering new ones in order to remain effective. One of the most common causes of lost sparring matches is predictable sparring. Avoid this by incorporating new ideas, strategies, and even new techniques into your sparring.

One way to do this is to incorporate techniques from other fighting arts. For example, learning how to box can improve the effectiveness of one's punches whether one spars Taekwondo or Karate style. You can watch a kickboxer to pick up pointers on timing. Any fighting art can yield plenty of examples for you to learn from and incorporate into your own sparring.

Boxing Techniques

Although most martial arts schools don't teach the techniques of boxing, they are good skills to have and will add considerably to your repertoire of martial arts techniques. You can practice these techniques on a heavy bag or in a shadow boxing workout. Adding some boxing drills will make your workouts more interesting and more productive. Understanding and practicing these techniques will make your other hand striking techniques better and more powerful. (And, since you might run into these techniques outside the training hall, they're good to know.)

The Basics

Spend some time practicing the fundamentals of boxing. The basics will take you a long way in sparring, so devote some time to them in every training session.

BOXING STANCE

Boxing techniques begin with a modified fighting stance. This is done by keeping one foot more forward than the other, as in a fighting stance. Both your feet and your body should face the target. (In a typical martial arts fighting stance, the chest and sometimes the hips are turned away.) In the boxing stance, your back shoulder should be turned slightly away. This makes you a smaller target and helps you generate more power. Stay light on your feet since you'll be pivoting frequently to make the most of your body power. Your hands should always be made into fists. Keep one fist on each side of your jaw. This protects you from knockout punches. Tuck your elbows in to protect your ribs from body blows.

JAB

The jab is a fast punch that is not necessarily intended to knock out the opponent. Use it to feel out the opponent's strengths and weaknesses and to see how the opponent will react to your punches. It can also be used to distract him or her. You might jab to the body to lower your opponent's guard and then quickly follow with another technique to the head, which will be unguarded.

Right-handed boxers jab with their left hand because they like to follow a jab with a stronger technique using their stronger arm. (Obviously, left-handed boxers have right-hand jabs.) But since martial arts emphasize balance, work both sides of your body equally. Practice both right- and left-hand jabs.

The jab is done with the hand that is on the same side as the forward foot. Instead of chambering your fist at the waist, as you do for martial arts punches, keep your jabbing fist at your jaw until you are ready to use it. Then, punch forward from your jaw, extending your elbow. Turn your body so that your shoulder goes into the punch as well. Pivot on your forward foot so that instead of pointing at your target, your toes are perpendicular to it at the time of impact. This helps generate additional power for maximum impact.

CROSS

The cross is a powerful punch that is usually done with the stronger arm. Practice with both hands to keep your practice balanced. The cross is performed with the arm on the same side as the back leg. It almost invariably follows the jab. Your fists should protect your jaw until you launch the punch. Drop your hand slightly so that your fist is facing your target. Punch forward, extending your elbow while turning your upper body into the blow. Both feet should pivot in the direction of the punch to add power.

HOOK

The hook is usually performed with the same hand as the jab. It uses the arm on the same side as the forward foot. The hook can also be executed using the back hand, although this is done less frequently. Cock the arm at the elbow at close to a 90-degree angle. Keep the cocked arm parallel to the floor. Pivot on your feet in the direction of the punch. Your arm should remain cocked as you swing your body forward. Don't extend your arm or straighten your elbow. Lead with your shoulder, which should turn toward the target with your cocked arm following. As you turn your body, your arm will hook or arc slightly forward, striking the target as you pivot. The shoulder always remains on the same plane as your chest.

UPPERCUT

The uppercut is usually performed with the same arm as the cross, that is, the arm on the same side as the back leg. The uppercut is a circular movement that strikes the target from underneath. It is done by keeping the fist near the jaw until you launch the punch. Then, reach slightly behind and drop your arm to waist level. Pivot into the punch. Extend your arm forward and up, striking the target with the top of your knuckles. The uppercut is often directed toward the midsection, but it can also be directed at the jaw, where it can be used to devastating effect.

Boxing Fundamentals

To master boxing techniques, practice them individually until you feel comfortable with them. Then put them together into punching combinations. Several elements are essential for good boxing technique. First, understand the mechanics. Your feet should pivot as you punch, which helps you get your body weight behind each technique. Always use your body—your chest and hips—not just your arms. Using only your arm generates very little power. For maximum impact, you must commit your whole body to the blow.

Finally, remember that although boxers usually develop one-sided techniques (the right-handed boxer jabs only with the left hand), martial artists shouldn't. If you practice jabs and other boxing techniques with both hands, you'll be able to deliver the punch no matter what foot is forward or what hand is punching. Make sure you practice each technique using each hand in order to gain true martial arts proficiency.

Timing

In boxing, timing requires the ability to feint and punch while avoiding blows. To practice boxing combinations, start simple.

Do several jabs in a row as if you were feeling out an opponent. Then suddenly add a cross. Repeat this combination several times. Once you have the rhythm of the jab-cross combination, add the hook. Once you have the rhythm of the jab-cross-hook combination, add the uppercut. Always remember to bring the punching hand back to the jaw. One hand should be up, protecting the jaw, at all times, even when an attack is being launched. Fighters who drop their nonpunching hand tend to get hit.

Speed

In boxing, speed is power. Try this: facing a heavy bag (or a partner holding a target), perform a cross. Hit as hard as you can, but don't draw your arm back. Let it remain against the bag for a moment or two. Repeat the cross a few times to get a sense of it.

Then, perform another kind of cross. Hit the target as hard as you can, but then draw your arm back as quickly as possible. Repeat this cross several times. You should notice a difference between the two. The fast cross is always more powerful than the slow cross.

To increase your hand speed, challenge yourself. Land a punch and pull it back quickly. Think of getting your fist back to protect your jaw as fast as possible. Once you can do this pretty quickly, add a twist by trying to land the next punch before your first punch is all the way back to your jaw. Try to increase the number of punches you can do this way without stopping.

To step up the difficulty level, have a partner hold two targets, one middle and the other high. Alternate striking them, still punching as quickly as possible.

Light Feet

Boxers must remain light on their feet. This helps them pivot into their punches and avoid their opponent's attacks. One way to work on "light feet" is to dance around a heavy bag (or simply move around in a small circle). Keep your feet in motion all the time, stopping only now and then to throw a punch. When you stop to strike, go ahead and lower your stance slightly to prevent being knocked back.

This drill is excellent for improving your footwork and will even help your kicking (light feet equals fast kicks), but remember that you can be penalized in sparring for circling. Martial artists who prefer not to practice circling can still practice light feet by using accepted martial arts footwork (forward stepping, back stepping, side stepping). To do this, face a target (real or imaginary). Quickly move forward and back and from side to side. At random, stop, plant, and launch

a punch or series of punches. Then resume the footwork. You can add kicks once you get a feel for the basic technique.

Bob-and-Weave

Practice the boxer's bob-and-weave by circling and ducking. Try to remain light on your feet by circling or using footwork. As an attack to your head (real or imagined) is launched, duck the blow. A partner can help by sweeping a hand target (or just a hand) in the direction of your jaw. Your goal is to duck and evade the hand. As your partner sweeps and you evade, follow up with a punch to the middle. Karate practitioners can punch high.

Using Techniques From Other Fighting Arts

You can learn from other fighting arts, not just boxing. Although you may not be able to incorporate the exact techniques (for example, an Aikido trap or joint lock isn't going to win you any points in Karate competition), you can nonetheless learn a great deal from other martial arts such as Muay Thai, Jujitsu, and Hapkido. The closer different martial arts are in technique and execution to your martial art form, the more you can use (Taekwondo and Karate practitioners, for example, steal each other's stuff all the time).

Even if a specific strike in another style isn't useful to you, perhaps that style uses footwork that you could incorporate or has body shifting techniques that you have never learned. Perhaps certain fighting concepts will be helpful to you.

By always watching what other martial artists do, you can improve your own fighting by adding the techniques and strategies that work best for you.

Tips for Strengthening Your Arsenal

Now that you've learned how to build up your arsenal with techniques from other fighting arts, it's time to learn how to hone these newfound skills. And remember, with sparring, your education continues throughout your life, so always be on the lookout for something new or a different approach that you might be able to use.

Keep Learning

Not only can you incorporate ideas from other martial arts, but you can learn a great deal from people in your own style. One key to becoming a better fighter is to observe and critique. Spar with different partners and ask them to rate or discuss your performance. Spar fighters who are willing to stop in the middle of a match and point out alternatives—what you could have done or should have done.

Videotape as many of your sparring matches as you can, both practice and competition, to see how they compare and to correct any weaknesses. Sometimes if you can identify and fix just one weakness, you will eliminate several other problems as well. For instance, if you put too much weight on your back leg, you will have difficulty doing reverse (back) kicks. So your correction is to distribute your weight more evenly. You will discover that doing so also improves your ability to avoid attacks by using footwork techniques. Such quick corrections can eliminate many seemingly serious problems and can vastly improve your skill level.

Observe as much martial arts performance as possible. Watch competitions (in person, on television, on video) to see what advanced fighters do. Read instructional articles and how-to books. When you see an impressive fighter or an impressive fight, focus on what works and why. If a fighter or a fight is less impressive, think about alternatives that would work better. Ask yourself what you would do differently. Try these sequences out with a partner, first as step sparring, then in your freestyle sparring.

Size Up Your Opponent

Understanding your opponent before the first strike lands is essential to success in sparring. Of course, the evaluation you make of an unknown fighter on first glance is going to be a superficial one, but you should be able to determine if your opponent is bigger and stronger or smaller and weaker (although bigger doesn't necessarily equate to stronger nor smaller to weaker). As a rule of thumb, bigger fighters will use more power techniques; smaller fighters will rely more on speed and agility. This means that you'll need to respond to different fighters in different ways. If you spar hard hitters the same way you spar light contact fighters or tall people the same way you spar short ones, you're not doing yourself any favors. Adjust your sparring to your opponent, but never let your opponent dictate the match.

If an opponent favors fast-paced, aggressive attacks, you won't be able to spar him or her the way you do an opponent who relies on countering techniques. You can't let your opponent control the match, but you should take his or her sparring tactics into consideration when planning your own strategy. Use countering techniques on aggressive fighters to score more easily, and don't commit yourself to easily countered techniques when sparring the counter fighter. In the section on timing, you saw that a reverse kick is easily countered with another reverse kick and that a roundhouse kick is easily countered with a reverse kick. The counter fighter is waiting for you to launch a reverse kick or a roundhouse kick for that very reason. Instead, use hand techniques. Or use the front kick, which can be blocked but is very hard to counter. Use double techniques in order to stop a counter fighter.

Within a few moments of a match, you should have some idea of what kind of opponent you are up against. Adjust your sparring accordingly and you'll be more likely to win the match.

Add Variety to Your Sparring

All martial artists have some techniques that work especially well for them. For one person, it might be a side kick. For another, it might be a backfist. Often, fighters rely on a select few tried-and-true techniques. While this makes sparring easier (because it is more automatic), it also makes it less successful. Add variety to your sparring repertoire and you'll improve your skills, overwhelm your opponents, and win matches.

Unpredictable sparring is essential to success. To help keep your sparring unpredictable, make a list of several of the most frequent techniques you use. Take the first technique on the list and stop using it. Instead, replace it with another technique that you don't use very often. Every time you plan to use your favored technique, use the new one instead. For example, if you like to use a roundhouse kick when you spar, plan to use a side kick instead. Every time you start to use your roundhouse kick, turn it into a side kick. Although this may slow you down at first, the effort is worth it. Once you've incorporated the side kick into your sparring, you can return the roundhouse kick to your arsenal—just don't use it so frequently. Then take the next favorite technique on your list and replace it. Continue going through your list until you are comfortable using a wide variety of techniques in a wide variety of circumstances.

Feinting

As you grow more skilled at sparring, you can set up scoring opportunities by feinting. This is the best way of feeling out an unknown opponent at the beginning of a match. If you feint with a roundhouse kick and your opponent immediately counters with a reverse kick, you will know you are sparring a counter fighter and should adjust your techniques accordingly. The feint does not commit you to the actual strike, so your opponent will probably be unable to score on you.

Using a feinting technique will also allow you to create openings that you can then attack. For example, suppose you begin a side kick by drawing your leg up to the chamber position and extending it slightly. Your partner may try to counter the side kick he or she sees by blocking it or by doing a reverse kick as a counter. By stopping your technique (feinting) you can get your opponent to commit to a block or kick. Once you see what counterattack your opponent has planned, you can respond by performing a technique of your own to an unguarded area, such as your partner's head. This sequence would go like this: you feint a side kick, wait until your partner leans forward to block, and then, while your opponent's hands and mind are occupied with the block, perform a roundhouse kick to the head. Feints can be used with any technique and can greatly improve your sparring practice.

Karate fighters often use feints to strike to high targets. For example, a fighter might feint a punch to the middle, drawing the opponent's guard down, then perform a backfist to the head. This middle-high tactic works with kicks as well. It can be especially successful with double kicks.

Learn From Your Mistakes

Learning from your mistakes can be challenging. It may be easy to see that your side kick gets blocked all the time, but it is not so easy to see how this can change. That's why you should get in the habit of talking with your sparring partners on a regular basis. If they see you perform techniques that don't work or that they repeatedly counter, they can tell you. They can also give you tips on how to fix that.

You should spend time evaluating your sparring and considering how to improve. This is where videotaping can come in handy. If every time you do a reverse kick your partner avoids it and counters with a reverse punch, ask yourself what you can change (other than never doing the reverse kick again). Perhaps you could do a reverse kick that only goes 180 degrees to confuse your opponent and make the reverse punch ineffective. Or maybe you could follow your first reverse kick quickly with a second reverse kick, which makes an excellent counter to a punch. Experiment with these changes and then incorporate them into your sparring.

Find Your Sparring Style

Most people, sooner or later, develop a characteristic sparring style. There is nothing wrong with this as long as you don't get predictable. For example, you may prefer to spar defensively. A defensive fighter has as much opportunity to win (a tournament, a brawl) as a fighter with an aggressive, offense-oriented approach. The more aggressive person might be spectacular to watch and might seem to take control of a match early, but such an opponent can be beaten by his or her own aggressiveness. Standing back and waiting for the opening that will surely come is one way to handle aggressive fighters. But the same goes for the defensive method. It may be that an aggressive opponent will defeat the defensive opponent simply by overwhelming him or her. One kind of fighting is not better than another. It depends on the martial artist (and to some extent, the opponents he or she meets).

Finding your sparring style doesn't mean that you don't try new techniques, new combinations, and new approaches as people suggest them to you or as you learn about them. Trying different methods helps you select the approach and basic techniques you'll always use. Incorporating new techniques helps add freshness and unpredictability to your fighting.

Identifying your sparring style helps you capitalize on your strengths, but don't dismiss suggestions and ideas because they don't seem to play to your strengths. At least consider new ideas, how they might apply, or how they could be adopted to suit your needs.

Nonetheless, you should have confidence in your style. Don't change it just because someone else considers it a bit unusual or thinks you would be more successful as another style of fighter. The more confident you are and the more you practice, the more you will develop the style that makes you the most effective martial artist you can be.

CHAPTER 11

THE PROGRAM

With practice, the martial artist has the ability to develop the self to its purest potential.

By following a sparring workout routine, you can hone your skills and become the best fighter possible. Several sample programs follow, but first you need to think about how you practice your freestyle sparring.

Practice, Practice, Practice

In the off-season, and for fun, you can freestyle spar according to whatever rules you and your partners decide on. But if you're preparing for a tournament, remember to practice according to tournament rules.

Recreating a tournament atmosphere as closely as possible can be very helpful. Begin by setting up a regulation-size sparring ring and recruiting someone to act as referee. Spar as if penalties were being assessed. For example, if you step out of bounds, have the referee call it, or notice it yourself. Use double-sided tape to mark the ring so you'll notice when you step on it.

If you compete in different tournaments with different rules, limit yourself to the techniques and target areas allowed by all. Then, a few weeks or days before each specific tournament, practice by those specific tournament rules.

In order to be ready to defend against a variety of techniques, have your partner spar according to different rules even as you spar to the more restricted tournament guidelines. On the same note, your partner can occasionally do illegal techniques (nothing dangerous), such as repeatedly kicking to your hip without warning. This can prepare you for unforeseen situations at a tournament. Although an opponent who uses illegal techniques in a tournament might be assessed a penalty, if you let yourself get frustrated or discouraged by it, your opponent will have won the match without scoring a point.

Try sparring with more equipment, less equipment, and no equipment to learn how to adjust to different equipment rules. Designate some practice matches as uniform contact only, others medium contact, and still others heavy contact (this does not mean that you and your partner should break each other's ribs).

Preparing for Unknown Opponents

As you practice for competition, your greatest challenge will be to prepare for unknown fighters. Most martial artists practice sparring with the same group of people all the time. This is useful because everyone plays by the same set of rules, but it can get you in trouble in competition, where you don't know what to expect.

Work with your partners to compensate for this. Design step sparring drills that use different techniques and sequences than the ones you and your partners are accustomed to doing. Vary your routine by designating some matches as kick-only (no hand strikes are allowed). Designate some matches hands-only. Or have your partner use only hand strikes while you use only kicks. This forces each fighter to be creative and to fight in different styles.

Changing Styles

Taekwondo and Karate fighters often enter each other's competitions because their styles are so similar. But enough differences exist that the Karate practitioner could get in trouble at the Taekwondo tournament, and vice versa. For instance, a Karate fighter might punch to the head, which would result in a penalty in a Taekwondo competition. The Taekwondo practitioner might do a spinning wheel kick to the head, which is illegal in some Karate tournaments. If you're interested in entering a different style tournament, read the corresponding section in this book and get a copy of the tournament rules sheet to practice by. Taekwondo techniques are covered in chapters 1 through 3, while Karate techniques are covered in chapters 4 through 6. Changing tournament sparring styles can be an exhilarating (although sometimes humbling) change of pace.

Sparring Workout

Devising a successful workout program to develop your sparring relies on your ability to assess your strengths and weaknesses. Once you have identified areas that need work (strength, for example, or flexibility), you can emphasize these parts of the workout. Of course, you must be sure not to neglect one area for the sake of another.

The following sparring workout is designed to enhance power, speed, and flexibility while improving sparring techniques and tactics.

Plan Your Workout

Ask These Questions:

How much time do I have to work out?

How have I worked out successfully in the past?

What do I want to achieve during my workout?

Do I have difficulty with certain martial arts techniques?

Identify Workout Goals:

To increase power, increase strength training segment.

To increase flexibility, increase stretching and flexibility drills.

To increase speed, increase speed and timing drills.

To improve timing, increase response drills and timing techniques.

To improve sparring, increase step sparring and combination drills.

Use the workout log on pages 188 and 189 to help you keep track of your workouts and monitor your progress.

TAEKWONDO WORKOUT: OFF-SEASON
BEGINNER

Duration: Workout should last about an hour, three or four times a week.

WARM-UP (5 MIN.)

Treadmill	(p. 121)
Jump rope	(p. 122)

STRETCHES (5 MIN.)

Neck stretch	(p. 122)	Open stretch	(p. 123)
Shoulder stretch	(p. 122)	Bicycle stretch	(p. 124)
Wrist stretch	(p. 122)	Hamstring stretch	(p. 124)
Back stretch	(p. 123)	Quadriceps stretch	(p. 124)
Hip flexor stretch	(p. 123)	Calf raises	(p. 124)
Groin stretch	(p. 123)		

STRENGTH TRAINING AND CONDITIONING (5-10 MIN.)

Weightlifting, if desired	(p. 125)	Push-ups (15×)	(p. 128)
Crunches (15×)	(p. 127)	Pull-ups (5 with spotter)	(p. 128)
Boxer sit-ups (15×)	(p. 127)	Slow motion kicks	
Rope-ups (15×)	(p. 128)	(15 sec. for each technique)	(p. 129)

FLEXIBILITY (5 MIN.)

Hamstring lift	(p. 130)	Chambering drill	
Groin lift	(p. 130)	(all kicks, 5× each leg)	(p. 130)

SPEED (5 MIN.)

Frog jumps (30 sec.)	(p. 131)	Hand response drill	
Jumping drill (8-12 in. or 20-30 cm high, 10×)	(p. 131)	(3-4 in. or 8-10 cm)	(p. 133)
Sweeping drill (8-12 in. or 20-30 cm high, 15×)	(p. 132)	Kick response drill (continue for 1 min.)	(p. 133)
Punching drill (50 punches in 30 sec.)	(p. 132)	Kick response variation (5×)	(p. 133)

TECHNIQUES PRACTICE (USING HEAVY BAG OR TARGET, 5-10 MIN.)

Punches

Straight punch	(p. 18)	Striking post drill	(p. 20)
Reverse punch	(p. 19)	Step-and-punch drill	(p. 20)

(continued)

Kicks

Front kick	(p. 22)	Roundhouse kick	(p. 23)
Side kick	(p. 22)	Reverse kick	(p. 24)

Blocks

Low block	(p. 35)	Blocking drill	(p. 38)
High block	(p. 35)		

TIMING TECHNIQUES (5 MIN.)

Punch block	(p. 136)	Reverse kick block	(p. 137)
Side kick block	(p. 136)	Punch against side kick	(p. 138)
Front kick block	(p. 137)	Punch against reverse kick	(p. 138)

BASIC COMBINATION DRILL (5 MIN.) (P. 143)

BOXING TECHNIQUES (2-MIN. ROUNDS AGAINST A HEAVY BAG)

Jab, cross, hook, uppercut	(p. 146)
Light feet drill	(p. 149)

STEP SPARRING (5 MIN.)

Counter with punches	(p. 45)	Counter with crescent kick and	
Counter with side kick	(p. 46)	hooking kick	(p. 47)

INFORMAL SPARRING PRACTICE (5-10 MIN.)

Heavy bag/shadow spar if no partner (p. 47)

COOL-DOWN

Focused breathing (1 min.)	(p. 117)
Visualization (3 min.)	(p. 117)

TAEKWONDO WORKOUT: OFF-SEASON
INTERMEDIATE

Duration: Workout should last about an hour, three or four times a week.

WARM-UP (5 MIN.)

Treadmill	(p. 121)		
Jump rope	(p. 122)		

STRETCHES (5 MIN.)

Neck stretch	(p. 122)	Open stretch	(p. 123)
Shoulder stretch	(p. 122)	Bicycle stretch	(p. 124)
Wrist stretch	(p. 122)	Hamstring stretch	(p. 124)
Back stretch	(p. 123)	Quadriceps stretch	(p. 124)
Hip flexor stretch	(p. 123)	Calf raises	(p. 124)
Groin stretch	(p. 123)		

STRENGTH TRAINING AND CONDITIONING (5-10 MIN.)

Weightlifting, if desired	(p. 125)	Push-ups (15×)	(p. 128)
Crunches (15×)	(p. 127)	Push-up variations 1, 2, and 3	
Crunch variations 1, 2, 3, and 4		(15× each)	(p. 128)
(15× each)	(p. 127)	Pull-ups (5 without spotter)	(p. 128)
Boxer sit-ups (30×)	(p. 127)	Slow motion kicks	
Rope-ups (30×)	(p. 128)	(30 sec. for each technique)	(p. 129)

FLEXIBILITY (5 MIN.)

Hamstring lift, with partner	(p. 130)	Chambering drill (all kicks,	
Groin lift, with partner	(p. 130)	5× each leg, waist high)	(p. 130)

SPEED (5 MIN.)

Frog jumps (45 sec.)	(p. 131)	Punching drill (60 punches in 30 sec.)	(p. 132)
Jumping drill (knee high, 15×,		Hand response drill (2-3 in. or 5-8 cm)	(p. 133)
no mistakes)	(p. 131)	Kick response drill	
Sweeping drill (knee high, 15×,		(continue for 90 sec.)	(p. 133)
no mistakes)	(p. 132)	Kick response variation (10×)	(p. 133)

TECHNIQUES PRACTICE (USING HEAVY BAG OR TARGET, 5-10 MIN.)

Punches:

Straight punch	(p. 18)	Striking post drill	(p. 20)
Reverse punch	(p. 19)	Step-and-punch drill	(p. 20)

(continued)

Kicks

Front kick	(p. 22)	Crescent kicks	(p. 25)
Side kick	(p. 22)	Double kick	(p. 24)
Roundhouse kick	(p. 23)	Hooking kick	(p. 27)
Reverse kick	(p. 24)	Speed kick drill	(p. 32)

Blocks

Low block	(p. 35)	Crescent blocks	(p. 36)
High block	(p. 35)	Blocking drill	(p. 38)

DEFENSIVE MANEUVERS

Body shifting drill	(p. 39)	Footwork drills	(p. 39)
Footwork practice	(p. 39)		

TIMING TECHNIQUES (5 MIN.)

Reverse kick against side kick	(p. 139)	Spinning wheel kick against spinning	
Reverse kick against reverse kick	(p. 140)	wheel kick	(p. 142)
Reverse kick against roundhouse kick	(p. 141)		

ADVANCED COMBINATION DRILL (VARIATION 1, 5 MIN.) (P. 143)

BOXING TECHNIQUES (2-MIN. ROUNDS AGAINST A HEAVY BAG)

Punch combinations	(p. 148)
Bob-and-weave	(p. 149)

STEP SPARRING (5 MIN.)

Counter with punches; add front kick	(p. 45)	Counter with crescent kick and	
Counter with side kick;		hooking kick; add roundhouse kick	(p. 47)
add reverse kick	(p. 46)		

INFORMAL SPARRING PRACTICE (5-10 MIN.)

Heavy bag/shadow spar if no partner (p. 47)

COOL-DOWN

Focused breathing (1 min.)	(p. 117)
Visualization (3 min.)	(p. 117)

TAEKWONDO WORKOUT: OFF-SEASON
ADVANCED

Duration: Workout should last about an hour, three or four times a week.

WARM-UP (5 MIN.)

Treadmill	(p. 121)
Jump rope	(p. 122)

STRETCHES (5 MIN.)

Neck stretch	(p. 122)	Open stretch	(p. 123)
Shoulder stretch	(p. 122)	Bicycle stretch	(p. 124)
Wrist stretch	(p. 122)	Hamstring stretch	(p. 124)
Back stretch	(p. 123)	Quadriceps stretch	(p. 124)
Hip flexor stretch	(p. 123)	Calf raises	(p. 124)
Groin stretch	(p. 123)	Stance stretches	(p. 125)

STRENGTH TRAINING AND CONDITIONING (5-10 MIN.)

Weightlifting, if desired	(p. 125)	Push-ups (20×)	(p. 128)
Crunches (20×)	(p. 127)	Push-up variations 1, 2, and 3	
Crunch variations 1, 2, 3, and 4		(20× each)	(p. 128)
(20× each)	(p. 127)	Pull-ups (10 without spotter)	(p. 128)
Boxer sit-ups (50×)	(p. 127)	Slow motion kicks	
Rope-ups (50×)	(p. 128)	(60 sec. for each technique)	(p. 129)

FLEXIBILITY (5 MIN.)

Hamstring lift, with partner		Chambering drill (all kicks,	
(hold 30-60 sec.)	(p. 130)	5× each leg, shoulder high)	(p. 130)
Groin lift, with partner (hold 30-60 sec.)	(p. 130)		

SPEED (5 MIN.)

Frog jumps (60 jumps in 60 sec.)	(p. 131)	Punching drill (75 punches in 30 sec.)	(p. 132)
Jumping drill (knee high, 20 jumps		Hand response drill (1-2 in. or 3-5 cm)	(p. 133)
in 30 sec., no mistakes)	(p. 131)	Kick response drill (continue for 2 min.)	(p. 133)
Sweeping drill (knee high, 30× in 30		Kick response variation (15×)	(p. 133)
sec., no mistakes)	(p. 132)		

TECHNIQUES PRACTICE (USING HEAVY BAG OR TARGET, 5-10 MIN.)

Punches

Straight punch	(p. 18)	Striking post drill	(p. 20)
Reverse punch	(p. 19)	Step-and-punch drill	(p. 20)

(continued)

Kicks

Front kick	(p. 22)	Jump side kick	(p. 29)
Side kick	(p. 22)	Jump front kick	(p. 29)
Roundhouse kick	(p. 23)	Jump reverse kick	(p. 30)
Reverse kick	(p. 24)	Jump roundhouse kick	(p. 30)
Crescent kicks	(p. 25)	Jump hooking kick	(p. 30)
Double kick	(p. 24)	Reverse jump hooking kick	(p. 31)
Hooking kick	(p. 27)	Speed kick drill	(p. 32)
Spinning wheel kick	(p. 28)		

Blocks

Low block	(p. 35)	Forearm block	(p. 37)
High block	(p. 35)	Blocking drill	(p. 38)
Crescent blocks	(p. 36)		

DEFENSIVE MANEUVERS (5 MIN.)

Body shifting drill	(p. 39)	Footwork drills	(p. 39)
Footwork practice	(p. 39)		

TIMING TECHNIQUES (5 MIN.)

Extended timing techniques	(p. 142)	Gear kicking	(p. 142)
Create own timing techniques	(p. 142)		

ADVANCED COMBINATION DRILL (VARIATION 2, 5 MIN.) (P. 144)

BOXING TECHNIQUES (2-MIN. ROUNDS AGAINST A HEAVY BAG)

Timing drill	(p. 148)	Two-target speed drill	(p. 149)
Speed drill	(p. 149)	Bob-and-weave; add punches	(p. 149)

STEP SPARRING (5 MIN.)

Create own step sparring sequences   (p. 44)

INFORMAL SPARRING PRACTICE (5-10 MIN.)

Heavy bag/shadow spar if no partner (p. 47)

COOL-DOWN

Focused breathing (1 min.)   (p. 117)
Visualization (3 min.)   (p. 117)

TAEKWONDO WORKOUT: TOURNAMENT SEASON

BEGINNER

Duration: Workout should last about an hour per session, six days per week.

Alternate the Conditioning Plan with the Sparring Plan. Monday, Wednesday, and Friday should be devoted to conditioning, with Tuesday, Thursday, and Saturday devoted to sparring.

CONDITIONING PLAN

WARM-UP (5 MIN.)

Treadmill	(p. 121)
Jump rope	(p. 122)

STRETCHES (5-10 MIN.)

Neck stretch	(p. 122)	Open stretch	(p. 123)
Shoulder stretch	(p. 122)	Bicycle stretch	(p. 124)
Wrist stretch	(p. 122)	Hamstring stretch	(p. 124)
Back stretch	(p. 123)	Quadriceps stretch	(p. 124)
Hip flexor stretch	(p. 123)	Calf raises	(p. 124)
Groin stretch	(p. 123)		

STRENGTH TRAINING AND CONDITIONING (20-30 MIN.)

Weightlifting	(p. 125)	Push-ups (15×)	(p. 128)
Crunches (15×)	(p. 127)	Pull-ups (5 with spotter)	(p. 128)
Boxer sit-ups (15×)	(p. 127)	Slow motion kicks	
Rope-ups (15×)	(p. 128)	(15 sec. for each technique)	(p. 129)

FLEXIBILITY (5-10 MIN.)

Hamstring lift	(p. 130)	Chambering drill	
Groin lift	(p. 130)	(all kicks, 5× each leg)	(p. 130)

SPEED (5-10 MIN.)

Frog jumps (30 sec.)	(p. 131)	Hand response drill	
Jumping drill (8-12 in. or 20-30 cm high, 10×)	(p. 131)	(3-4 in. or 8-10 cm)	(p. 133)
Sweeping drill (8-12 in. or 20-30 cm high, 15×)	(p. 132)	Kick response drill (continue for 1 min.)	(p. 133)
Punching drill (50 punches in 30 sec.)	(p. 132)	Kick response variation (5×)	(p. 133)

SPARRING PLAN

WARM-UP (5 MIN.)

Treadmill	(p. 121)
Jump rope	(p. 122)

(continued)

STRETCHES (5 MIN.)

Neck stretch	(p. 122)	Open stretch	(p. 123)
Shoulder stretch	(p. 122)	Bicycle stretch	(p. 124)
Wrist stretch	(p. 122)	Hamstring stretch	(p. 124)
Back stretch	(p. 123)	Quadriceps stretch	(p. 124)
Hip flexor stretch	(p. 123)	Calf raises	(p. 124)
Groin stretch	(p. 123)		

TECHNIQUES PRACTICE (USING HEAVY BAG OR TARGET, 5-10 MIN.)

Punches

Straight punch	(p. 18)	Striking post drill	(p. 20)
Reverse punch	(p. 19)	Step-and-punch drill	(p. 20)

Kicks

Front kick	(p. 22)	Roundhouse kick	(p. 23)
Side kick	(p. 22)	Reverse kick	(p. 24)

Blocks

Low block	(p. 35)	Blocking drill	(p. 38)
High block	(p. 35)		

TIMING TECHNIQUES (5-10 MIN.)

Punch block	(p. 136)	Reverse kick block	(p. 137)
Side kick block	(p. 136)	Punch against side kick	(p. 138)
Front kick block	(p. 137)	Punch against reverse kick	(p. 138)

BASIC COMBINATION DRILL (5 MIN.) (P. 143)

BOXING TECHNIQUES (2-MIN. ROUNDS AGAINST A HEAVY BAG)

Jab, cross, hook, uppercut	(p. 146)
Light feet drill	(p. 149)

STEP SPARRING (5 MIN.)

Counter with punches	(p. 45)	Counter with crescent kick	
Counter with side kick	(p. 46)	and hooking kick	(p. 47)

FORMAL TOURNAMENT SPARRING PRACTICE (10-20 MIN.) (P. 47)

COOL-DOWN

Focused breathing (1 min.)	(p. 117)
Visualization (3 min.)	(p. 117)

TAEKWONDO WORKOUT: TOURNAMENT SEASON
INTERMEDIATE

Duration: Workout should last about an hour per session, six days per week.

Alternate the Conditioning Plan with the Sparring Plan. Monday, Wednesday, and Friday should be devoted to conditioning, with Tuesday, Thursday, and Saturday devoted to sparring.

CONDITIONING PLAN

WARM-UP (5 MIN.)

Treadmill	(p. 121)
Jump rope	(p. 122)

STRETCHES (5-10 MIN.)

Neck stretch	(p. 122)	Open stretch	(p. 123)
Shoulder stretch	(p. 122)	Bicycle stretch	(p. 124)
Wrist stretch	(p. 122)	Hamstring stretch	(p. 124)
Back stretch	(p. 123)	Quadriceps stretch	(p. 124)
Hip flexor stretch	(p. 123)	Calf raises	(p. 124)
Groin stretch	(p. 123)	Stance stretches	(p. 125)

STRENGTH TRAINING AND CONDITIONING (20-30 MIN.)

Weightlifting	(p. 125)	Push-ups (15×)	(p. 128)
Crunches (15×)	(p. 127)	Push-up variations 1, 2, and 3	
Crunch variations 1, 2, 3, and 4		(15× each)	(p. 128)
(15× each)	(p. 127)	Pull-ups (5 without spotter)	(p. 128)
Boxer sit-ups (30×)	(p. 127)	Slow motion kicks	
Rope-ups (30×)	(p. 128)	(30 sec. for each technique)	(p. 129)

FLEXIBILITY (5-10 MIN.)

Hamstring lift, with partner	(p. 130)	Chambering drill (all kicks, 5× each leg,	
Groin lift, with partner	(p. 130)	waist high)	(p. 130)

SPEED (5-10 MIN.)

Frog jumps (45 sec.)	(p. 131)	Hand response drill	
Jumping drill		(2-3 in. or 5-8 cm)	(p. 133)
(knee high, 15×, no mistakes)	(p. 131)	Kick response drill	
Sweeping drill		(continue for 90 sec.)	(p. 133)
(knee high, 15×, no mistakes)	(p. 132)	Kick response variation (10×)	(p. 133)
Punching drill			
(60 punches in 30 sec.)	(p. 132)		

(continued)

SPARRING PLAN

WARM-UP (5 MIN.)

Treadmill	(p. 121)		
Jump rope	(p. 122)		

STRETCHES (5-10 MIN.)

Neck stretch	(p. 122)	Open stretch	(p. 123)
Shoulder stretch	(p. 122)	Bicycle stretch	(p. 124)
Wrist stretch	(p. 122)	Hamstring stretch	(p. 124)
Back stretch	(p. 123)	Quadriceps stretch	(p. 124)
Hip flexor stretch	(p. 123)	Calf raises	(p. 124)
Groin stretch	(p. 123)		

TECHNIQUES PRACTICE (USING HEAVY BAG OR TARGET, 5-10 MIN.)

Punches

Straight punch	(p. 18)	Striking post drill	(p. 20)
Reverse punch	(p. 19)	Step-and-punch drill	(p. 20)

Kicks

Front kick	(p. 22)	Crescent kicks	(p. 25)
Side kick	(p. 22)	Double kick	(p. 24)
Roundhouse kick	(p. 23)	Hooking kick	(p. 27)
Reverse kick	(p. 24)	Speed kick drill	(p. 32)

Blocks

Low block	(p. 35)	Crescent blocks	(p. 36)
High block	(p. 35)	Blocking drill	(p. 38)

DEFENSIVE MANEUVERS (5 MIN.)

Body shifting drill	(p. 39)	Footwork drills	(p. 39)
Footwork practice	(p. 39)		

TAEKWONDO WORKOUT: TOURNAMENT SEASON
INTERMEDIATE *(continued)*

TIMING TECHNIQUES (5-10 MIN.)

Reverse kick against side kick (p. 139)

Reverse kick against reverse kick (p. 140)

Reverse kick against
roundhouse kick (p. 141)

Spinning wheel kick against spinning
wheel kick (p. 142)

ADVANCED COMBINATION DRILL (VARIATION 1, 5 MIN.) (P. 143)

BOXING TECHNIQUES (2-MIN. ROUNDS AGAINST A HEAVY BAG)

Punch combinations (p. 148)

Bob-and-weave (p. 149)

STEP SPARRING (5 MIN.)

Counter with punches; add front kick (p. 45)

Counter with side kick;
add reverse kick (p. 46)

Counter with crescent kick and hooking
kick; add roundhouse kick (p. 47)

FORMAL TOURNAMENT SPARRING PRACTICE (10-20 MIN.) (P. 47)

COOL-DOWN

Focused breathing (1 min.) (p. 117)

Visualization (3 min.) (p. 117)

TAEKWONDO WORKOUT: TOURNAMENT SEASON

ADVANCED

Duration: Workout should last about an hour per session, six days per week.

Alternate the Conditioning Plan with the Sparring Plan. Monday, Wednesday, and Friday should be devoted to conditioning, with Tuesday, Thursday, and Saturday devoted to sparring.

CONDITIONING PLAN

WARM-UP (5 MIN.)

Treadmill	(p. 121)	
Jump rope	(p. 122)	

STRETCHES (5-10 MIN.)

Neck stretch	(p. 122)	Open stretch	(p. 123)
Shoulder stretch	(p. 122)	Bicycle stretch	(p. 124)
Wrist stretch	(p. 122)	Hamstring stretch	(p. 124)
Back stretch	(p. 123)	Quadriceps stretch	(p. 124)
Hip flexor stretch	(p. 123)	Calf raises	(p. 124)
Groin stretch	(p. 123)	Stance stretches	(p. 125)

STRENGTH TRAINING AND CONDITIONING (20-30 MIN.)

Weightlifting	(p. 125)	Push-ups (20×)	(p. 128)
Crunches (20×)	(p. 127)	Push-up variations 1, 2, and 3	
Crunch variations 1, 2, 3, and 4		(20× each)	(p. 128)
(20× each)	(p. 127)	Pull-ups (10 without spotter)	(p. 128)
Boxer sit-ups (50×)	(p. 127)	Slow motion kicks	
Rope-ups (50×)	(p. 128)	(60 sec. for each technique)	(p. 129)

FLEXIBILITY (5-10 MIN.)

Hamstring lift, with partner		Chambering drill (all kicks,	
(hold 30-60 sec.)	(p. 130)	5× each leg, shoulder high)	(p. 130)
Groin lift, with partner			
(hold 30-60 sec.)	(p. 130)		

SPEED (5-10 MIN.)

Frog jumps (60 jumps in 60 sec.)	(p. 131)	Punching drill (75 punches in 30 sec.)	(p. 132)
Jumping drill (knee high,		Hand response drill (1-2 in. or 3-5 cm)	(p. 133)
20 jumps in 30 sec., no mistakes)	(p. 131)	Kick response drill	
Sweeping drill (knee high,		(continue for 2 min.)	(p. 133)
30× in 30 sec., no mistakes)	(p. 132)	Kick response variation (15×)	(p. 133)

SPARRING PLAN

WARM-UP (5 MIN.)

Treadmill	(p. 121)	
Jump rope	(p. 122)	

STRETCHES (5-10 MIN.)

Neck stretch	(p. 122)	Open stretch	(p. 123)
Shoulder stretch	(p. 122)	Bicycle stretch	(p. 124)
Wrist stretch	(p. 122)	Hamstring stretch	(p. 124)
Back stretch	(p. 123)	Quadriceps stretch	(p. 124)
Hip flexor stretch	(p. 123)	Calf raises	(p. 124)
Groin stretch	(p. 123)	Stance stretches	(p. 125)

TECHNIQUES PRACTICE (USING HEAVY BAG OR TARGET, 5-10 MIN.)

Punches

Straight punch	(p. 18)	Striking post drill	(p. 20)
Reverse punch	(p. 19)	Step-and-punch drill	(p. 20)

Kicks

Front kick	(p. 22)	Jump side kick	(p. 29)
Side kick	(p. 22)	Jump front kick	(p. 29)
Roundhouse kick	(p. 23)	Jump reverse kick	(p. 30)
Reverse kick	(p. 24)	Jump roundhouse kick	(p. 30)
Crescent kicks	(p. 25)	Jump hooking kick	(p. 30)
Double kick	(p. 24)	Reverse jump hooking kick	(p. 31)
Hooking kick	(p. 27)	Speed kick drill	(p. 32)
Spinning wheel kick	(p. 28)		

Blocks

Low block	(p. 35)	Forearm block	(p. 37)
High block	(p. 35)	Blocking drill	(p. 38)
Crescent blocks	(p. 36)		

DEFENSIVE MANEUVERS (5 MIN.)

Body shifting drill	(p. 39)	Footwork drills	(p. 39)
Footwork practice	(p. 39)		

(continued)

TAEKWONDO WORKOUT: TOURNAMENT SEASON

ADVANCED *(continued)*

TIMING TECHNIQUES (5-10 MIN.)

Extended timing techniques	(p. 142)	Gear kicking	(p. 142)
Create own timing techniques	(p. 142)		

ADVANCED COMBINATION DRILL (VARIATION 2, 5 MIN.) (P. 144)

BOXING TECHNIQUES (2-MIN. ROUNDS AGAINST A HEAVY BAG)

Timing drill	(p. 148)	Two-target speed drill	(p. 149)
Speed drill	(p. 149)	Bob-and-weave; add punches	(p. 149)

STEP SPARRING (5 MIN.)

Create own step sparring sequences (p. 44)

FORMAL TOURNAMENT SPARRING PRACTICE (10-20 MIN.) (P. 47)

COOL-DOWN

Focused breathing (1 min.)	(p. 117)
Visualization (3 min.)	(p. 117)

KARATE WORKOUT: OFF-SEASON
BEGINNER

Duration: Workout should last about an hour, three or four times a week.

WARM-UP (5 MIN.)

Treadmill	(p. 121)		
Jump rope	(p. 122)		

STRETCHES (5 MIN.)

Neck stretch	(p. 122)	Back stretch	(p. 123)
Shoulder stretch	(p. 122)	Hip flexor stretch	(p. 123)
Wrist stretch	(p. 122)	Groin stretch	(p. 123)

STRENGTH TRAINING AND CONDITIONING (5-10 MIN.)

Weightlifting, if desired	(p. 125)	Boxer sit-ups (15×)	(p. 127)
Crunches (15×)	(p. 127)	Rope-ups (15×)	(p. 128)

FLEXIBILITY (5 MIN.)

Hamstring lift	(p. 130)		
Groin lift	(p. 130)		

SPEED (5 MIN.)

Frog jumps (30 sec.)	(p. 131)	Sweeping drill (8-12 in. or 20-30 cm high, 15×)	(p. 132)
Jumping drill (8-12 in. or 20-30 cm high, 10×)	(p. 131)	Punching drill (50 punches in 30 sec.)	(p. 132)

TECHNIQUES PRACTICE (USING HEAVY BAG OR TARGET, 5-10 MIN.)

Punches

Forefist	(p. 65)	Reverse punch	(p. 66)
Straight punch	(p. 66)		

Kicks

Front kick	(p. 74)	Roundhouse kick	(p. 77)
Crescent kicks	(p. 75)	Back kick	(p. 77)
Side kick	(p. 76)		

Elbow strikes

Forward	(p. 82)	Downward	(p. 83)
Reverse	(p. 82)	Side	(p. 84)
Upward	(p. 83)		

Knee strikes

Straight knee	(p. 84)		
Roundhouse knee	(p. 85)		

(continued)

Takedowns, throws, and sweeps

Shoulder takedown	(p. 87)	Hip throw	(p. 89)
Elbow takedown	(p. 88)		

Blocks

Downward block	(p. 91)	Crescent blocks	(p. 92)
Upper block	(p. 91)	Blocking drill	(p. 94)

TIMING TECHNIQUES (5 MIN.)

Punch block	(p. 136)	Reverse kick block	(p. 137)
Side kick block	(p. 136)	Punch against side kick	(p. 138)
Front kick block	(p. 137)	Punch against reverse kick	(p. 138)

BASIC COMBINATION DRILL (5 MIN.) (P. 143)

BOXING TECHNIQUES (2-MIN. ROUNDS AGAINST A HEAVY BAG)

Jab, cross, hook, uppercut	(p. 146)
Light feet drill	(p. 149)

STEP SPARRING (5 MIN.)

Counter with hand techniques	(p. 101)	Counter with double kick	(p. 102)
Counter with hand strike and elbow strike	(p. 101)		

INFORMAL SPARRING PRACTICE (5-10 MIN.)

Heavy bag/shadow spar if no partner (p. 103)

COOL-DOWN

Focused breathing. (1 min.)	(p. 117)
Visualization. (3 min.)	(p. 117)

KARATE WORKOUT: OFF-SEASON
INTERMEDIATE

Duration: Workout should last about an hour, three or four times a week.

WARM-UP (5 MIN.)

Treadmill	(p. 121)		
Jump rope	(p. 122)		

STRETCHES (5 MIN.)

Neck stretch	(p. 122)	Open stretch	(p. 123)
Shoulder stretch	(p. 122)	Bicycle stretch	(p. 124)
Wrist stretch	(p. 122)	Hamstring stretch	(p. 124)
Back stretch	(p. 123)	Quadriceps stretch	(p. 124)
Hip flexor stretch	(p. 123)	Calf raises	(p. 124)
Groin stretch	(p. 123)		

STRENGTH TRAINING AND CONDITIONING (5-10 MIN.)

Weightlifting, if desired	(p. 125)	Push-ups (15×)	(p. 128)
Crunches (15×)	(p. 127)	Push-up variations 1, 2, and 3	
Crunch variations 1, 2, 3, and 4		(15× each)	(p. 128)
(15× each)	(p. 127)	Pull-ups (5 without spotter)	(p. 128)
Boxer sit-ups (30×)	(p. 127)	Slow motion kicks	
Rope-ups (30×)	(p. 128)	(30 sec. for each technique)	(p. 129)

FLEXIBILITY (5 MIN.)

Hamstring lift, with partner	(p. 130)	Chambering drill (all kicks,	
Groin lift, with partner	(p. 130)	5× each leg, waist high)	(p. 130)

SPEED (5 MIN.)

Frog jumps (45 sec.)	(p. 131)	Punching drill (60 punches in 30 sec.)	(p. 132)
Jumping drill (knee high, 15×,		Hand response drill (2-3 in. or 5-8 cm)	(p. 133)
no mistakes)	(p. 131)	Kick response drill	
Sweeping drill (knee high, 15×,		(continue for 90 sec.)	(p. 133)
no mistakes)	(p. 132)	Kick response variation (10×)	(p. 133)

TECHNIQUES PRACTICE (USING HEAVY BAG OR TARGET, 5-10 MIN.)

Punches

Forefist	(p. 65)	Double punch	(p. 67)
Straight punch	(p. 66)	Striking post drill	(p. 71)
Reverse punch	(p. 66)	Step-and-punch drill	(p. 73)

(continued)

Hand Strikes

Knife hand strike	(p. 67)	Backfist	(p. 70)
Ridge hand strike	(p. 68)	Downward hammer fist strike	(p. 70)
Reverse ridge hand strike	(p. 69)	Horizontal hammer fist strike	(p. 71)
Palm strike	(p. 69)		

Kicks

Front kick	(p. 74)	Double kick	(p. 80)
Side kick	(p. 76)	Speed kick drill	(p. 81)
Roundhouse kick	(p. 77)	Step kick	(p. 79)
Crescent kicks	(p. 75)	Back kick	(p. 77)

Elbow strikes

Forward	(p. 82)	Downward	(p. 83)
Reverse	(p. 82)	Side	(p. 84)
Upward	(p. 83)		

Knee strikes

Straight knee	(p. 84)	Elbow and knee speed drill	(p. 85)
Roundhouse knee	(p. 85)		

Takedowns, throws, and sweeps

Shoulder takedown	(p. 87)	Takedown countering	
Elbow takedown	(p. 88)	roundhouse kick	(p. 90)
Hip throw	(p. 89)		

Blocks

Downward block	(p. 91)	Blocking drill	(p. 94)
Upper block	(p. 91)	Foot and leg blocks	(p. 93)
Crescent blocks	(p. 92)		

DEFENSIVE MANEUVERS (5 MIN.)

Body shifting drill	(p. 94)	Footwork drills	(p. 95)
Footwork practice	(p. 95)		

TIMING TECHNIQUES (5 MIN.)

Reverse kick against side kick	(p. 139)	Reverse kick against	
Reverse kick against reverse kick	(p. 140)	roundhouse kick	(p. 141)

ADVANCED COMBINATION DRILL (VARIATION 1, 5 MIN.) (P. 143)

BOXING TECHNIQUES (2-MIN. ROUNDS AGAINST A HEAVY BAG)

Punch combinations	(p. 148)
Bob-and-weave	(p. 149)

STEP SPARRING (5 MIN.)

Counter with hand techniques; add front kick	(p. 101)	Counter with double kick; add front kick; add middle-high double kick	(p. 102)
Counter with hand strike and elbow strike; add knee strike	(p. 101)		

INFORMAL SPARRING PRACTICE (5-10 MIN.)

Heavy bag/shadow spar if no partner	(p. 103)

COOL-DOWN

Focused breathing (1 min.)	(p. 117)
Visualization (3 min.)	(p. 117)

KARATE WORKOUT: OFF-SEASON
ADVANCED

Duration: Workout should last about an hour, three or four times a week.

WARM-UP (5 MIN.)

Treadmill	(p. 121)		
Jump rope	(p. 122)		

STRETCHES (5 MIN.)

Neck stretch	(p. 122)	Open stretch	(p. 123)
Shoulder stretch	(p. 122)	Bicycle stretch	(p. 124)
Wrist stretch	(p. 122)	Hamstring stretch	(p. 124)
Back stretch	(p. 123)	Quadriceps stretch	(p. 124)
Hip flexor stretch	(p. 123)	Calf raises	(p. 124)
Groin stretch	(p. 123)		

STRENGTH TRAINING AND CONDITIONING (5-10 MIN.)

Weightlifting, if desired	(p. 125)	Push-ups (15×)	(p. 128)
Crunches (15×)	(p. 127)	Push-up variations 1, 2, and 3	
Crunch variations 1, 2, 3, and 4		(15× each)	(p. 128)
(15× each)	(p. 127)	Pull-ups (5 without spotter)	(p. 128)
Boxer sit-ups (30×)	(p. 127)	Slow motion kicks (30 sec.	
Rope-ups (30×)	(p. 128)	for each technique)	(p. 129)

FLEXIBILITY (5 MIN.)

Hamstring lift, with partner	(p. 130)	Chambering drill (all kicks,	
Groin lift, with partner	(p. 130)	5× each leg, waist high)	(p. 130)

SPEED (5 MIN.)

Frog jumps (45 sec.)	(p. 131)	Punching drill (60 punches in 30 sec.)	(p. 132)
Jumping drill (knee high, 15×,		Hand response drill (1-2 in. or 3-5 cm)	(p. 133)
no mistakes)	(p. 131)	Kick response drill (continue	
Sweeping drill (knee high, 15×,		for 90 sec.)	(p. 133)
no mistakes)	(p. 132)	Kick response variation (10×)	(p. 133)

TECHNIQUES PRACTICE (USING HEAVY BAG OR TARGET, 5-10 MIN.)

Punches

Forefist	(p. 65)	Double punch	(p. 67)
Straight punch	(p. 66)	Striking post drill	(p. 71)
Reverse punch	(p. 66)	Step-and-punch drill	(p. 73)

Hand Strikes

Knife hand strike	(p. 67)	Backfist	(p. 70)
Ridge hand strike	(p. 68)	Downward hammer fist strike	(p. 70)
Reverse ridge hand strike	(p. 69)	Horizontal hammer fist strike	(p. 71)
Palm strike	(p. 69)	Double hand strike	(p. 67)

Kicks

Front kick	(p. 74)	Speed kick drill	(p. 81)
Side kick	(p. 76)	Step kick	(p. 79)
Roundhouse kick	(p. 77)	Back kick	(p. 77)
Crescent kicks	(p. 75)	Jumping kicks	(p. 78)
Double kick	(p. 80)		

Elbow strikes

Forward	(p. 82)	Downward	(p. 83)
Reverse	(p. 82)	Side	(p. 84)
Upward	(p. 83)		

Knee strikes

Straight knee	(p. 84)	Elbow and knee speed drill	(p. 85)
Roundhouse knee	(p. 85)		

Takedowns, throws, and sweeps

Shoulder takedown	(p. 87)	Takedown countering	
Elbow takedown	(p. 88)	roundhouse kick	(p. 90)
Hip throw	(p. 89)		

Blocks

Downward block	(p. 91)	Blocking drill	(p. 94)
Upper block	(p. 92)	Foot and leg blocks	(p. 93)
Crescent blocks	(p. 92)		

DEFENSIVE MANEUVERS (5 MIN.)

Body shifting drill	(p. 94)	Footwork drills	(p. 95)
Footwork practice	(p. 95)		

TIMING TECHNIQUES (5 MIN.)

Reverse kick against side kick	(p. 139)	Reverse kick against	
Reverse kick against reverse kick	(p. 140)	roundhouse kick	(p. 141)

(continued)

ADVANCED COMBINATION DRILL (VARIATION 1, 5 MIN.) (P. 143)

BOXING TECHNIQUES (2-MIN. ROUNDS AGAINST A HEAVY BAG)

Punch combinations   (p. 148)
Bob-and-weave   (p. 149)

STEP SPARRING (5 MIN.)

Create own step sparring sequences (p. 100)

INFORMAL SPARRING PRACTICE (5-10 MIN.)

Heavy bag/shadow spar if no partner (p. 103)

COOL-DOWN

Focused breathing (1 min.)   (p. 117)
Visualization (3 min.)   (p. 117)

KARATE WORKOUT: TOURNAMENT SEASON
BEGINNER

Duration: Workout should last about an hour per session, six days per week.

Alternate the Conditioning Plan with the Sparring Plan. Monday, Wednesday, and Friday should be devoted to conditioning, with Tuesday, Thursday, and Saturday devoted to sparring.

CONDITIONING PLAN

WARM-UP (5 MIN.)

Treadmill	(p. 121)		
Jump rope	(p. 122)		

STRETCHES (5-10 MIN.)

Neck stretch	(p. 122)	Open stretch	(p. 123)
Shoulder stretch	(p. 122)	Bicycle stretch	(p. 124)
Wrist stretch	(p. 122)	Hamstring stretch	(p. 124)
Back stretch	(p. 123)	Quadriceps stretch	(p. 124)
Hip flexor stretch	(p. 123)	Calf raises	(p. 124)
Groin stretch	(p. 123)		

STRENGTH TRAINING AND CONDITIONING (20-30 MIN.)

Weightlifting	(p. 125)	Push-ups (15×)	(p. 128)
Crunches (15×)	(p. 127)	Pull-ups (5 with spotter)	(p. 128)
Boxer sit-ups (15×)	(p. 127)	Slow motion kicks	
Rope-ups (15×)	(p. 128)	(15 sec. for each technique)	(p. 129)

FLEXIBILITY (5-10 MIN.)

Hamstring lift	(p. 130)	Chambering drill (all kicks,	
Groin lift	(p. 130)	5× each leg)	(p. 130)

SPEED (5-10 MIN.)

Frog jumps (30 sec.)	(p. 131)	Hand response drill (3-4 in.	
Jumping drill (8-12 in. or 20-30 cm		or 8-10 cm)	(p. 133)
high, 10×)	(p. 131)	Kick response drill (continue	
Sweeping drill (8-12 in.		for 1 min.)	(p. 133)
or 20-30 cm high, 15×)	(p. 132)	Kick response variation (5×)	(p. 133)
Punching drill (50 punches			
in 30 sec.)	(p. 132)		

(continued)

SPARRING PLAN

WARM-UP (5 MIN.)

Treadmill	(p. 121)
Jump rope	(p. 122)

STRETCHES (5 MIN.)

Neck stretch	(p. 122)	Open stretch	(p. 123)
Shoulder stretch	(p. 122)	Bicycle stretch	(p. 124)
Wrist stretch	(p. 122)	Hamstring stretch	(p. 124)
Back stretch	(p. 123)	Quadriceps stretch	(p. 124)
Hip flexor stretch	(p. 123)	Calf raises	(p. 124)
Groin stretch	(p. 123)		

TECHNIQUES PRACTICE (USING HEAVY BAG OR TARGET, 10-15 MIN.)

Punches

Forefist	(p. 65)	Striking post drill	(p. 71)
Straight punch	(p. 66)	Step-and-punch drill	(p. 73)
Reverse punch	(p. 66)		

Kicks

Front kick	(p. 74)	Roundhouse kick	(p. 77)
Crescent kicks	(p. 75)	Back kick	(p. 77)
Side kick	(p. 76)		

Elbow strikes

Forward	(p. 82)	Downward	(p. 83)
Reverse	(p. 82)	Side	(p. 84)
Upward	(p. 83)		

Knee strikes:

Straight knee	(p. 84)
Roundhouse knee	(p. 85)

Takedowns, throws, and sweeps:

Shoulder takedown	(p. 87)	Hip throw	(p. 89)
Elbow takedown	(p. 88)		

Blocks:

Downward block	(p. 91)	Crescent blocks	(p. 92)
Upper block	(p. 91)	Blocking drill	(p. 94)

TIMING TECHNIQUES (5-10 MIN.)

Punch block	(p. 136)	Reverse kick block	(p. 137)
Side kick block	(p. 136)	Punch against side kick	(p. 138)
Front kick block	(p. 137)	Punch against reverse kick	(p. 138)

BASIC COMBINATION DRILL (5 MIN.) (P. 143)

BOXING TECHNIQUES (2-MIN. ROUNDS AGAINST A HEAVY BAG)

Jab, cross, hook, uppercut	(p. 146)
Light feet drill	(p. 149)

STEP SPARRING (5 MIN.)

Counter with hand techniques	(p. 101)	Counter with double kick	(p. 102)
Counter with hand strike and elbow strike	(p. 101)		

INFORMAL SPARRING PRACTICE (10-20 MIN.)

Heavy bag/shadow spar if no partner	(p. 103)

COOL-DOWN

Focused breathing (1 min.)	(p. 117)
Visualization (3 min.)	(p. 117)

KARATE WORKOUT: TOURNAMENT SEASON
INTERMEDIATE

Duration: Workout should last about an hour per session, six days per week.

Alternate the Conditioning Plan with the Sparring Plan. Monday, Wednesday, and Friday should be devoted to conditioning, with Tuesday, Thursday, and Saturday devoted to sparring.

CONDITIONING PLAN

WARM-UP (5 MIN.)

Treadmill	(p. 121)
Jump rope	(p. 122)

STRETCHES (5-10 MIN.)

Neck stretch	(p. 122)	Open stretch	(p. 123)
Shoulder stretch	(p. 122)	Bicycle stretch	(p. 124)
Wrist stretch	(p. 122)	Hamstring stretch	(p. 124)
Back stretch	(p. 123)	Quadriceps stretch	(p. 124)
Hip flexor stretch	(p. 123)	Calf raises	(p. 124)
Groin stretch	(p. 123)		

STRENGTH TRAINING AND CONDITIONING (20-30 MIN.)

Weightlifting, if desired	(p. 125)	Push-ups (15×)	(p. 128)
Crunches (15×)	(p. 127)	Push-up variations 1, 2, and 3	
Crunch variations 1, 2, 3, and 4		(15× each)	(p. 128)
(15× each)	(p. 127)	Pull-ups (5 without spotter)	(p. 128)
Boxer sit-ups (30×)	(p. 127)	Slow motion kicks	
Rope-ups (30×)	(p. 128)	(30 sec. for each technique)	(p. 129)

FLEXIBILITY (5-10 MIN.)

Hamstring lift, with partner	(p. 130)	Chambering drill (all kicks,	
Groin lift, with partner	(p. 130)	5× each leg, waist high)	(p. 130)

SPEED (5-10 MIN.)

Frog jumps (45 sec.)	(p. 131)	Hand response drill (2-3 in.	
Jumping drill (knee high, 15×,		or 5-8 cm)	(p. 133)
no mistakes)	(p. 131)	Kick response drill (continue	
Sweeping drill (knee high, 15×,		for 90 sec.)	(p. 133)
no mistakes)	(p. 132)	Kick response variation (10×)	(p. 133)
Punching drill (60 punches			
in 30 sec.)	(p. 132)		

SPARRING PLAN

WARM-UP (5 MIN.)

Treadmill	(p. 121)
Jump rope	(p. 122)

STRETCHES (5 MIN.)

Neck stretch	(p. 122)	Open stretch	(p. 123)
Shoulder stretch	(p. 122)	Bicycle stretch	(p. 124)
Wrist stretch	(p. 122)	Hamstring stretch	(p. 124)
Back stretch	(p. 123)	Quadriceps stretch	(p. 124)
Hip flexor stretch	(p. 123)	Calf raises	(p. 124)
Groin stretch	(p. 123)		

TECHNIQUES PRACTICE (USING HEAVY BAG OR TARGET, 10-15 MIN.)

Punches

Forefist	(p. 65)	Double punch	(p. 67)
Straight punch	(p. 66)	Striking post drill	(p. 71)
Reverse punch	(p. 66)	Step-and-punch drill	(p. 73)

Hand Strikes

Knife hand strike	(p. 67)	Backfist	(p. 70)
Ridge hand strike	(p. 68)	Downward hammer fist strike	(p. 70)
Reverse ridge hand strike	(p. 69)	Horizontal hammer fist strike	(p. 71)
Palm strike	(p. 69)		

Kicks

Front kick	(p. 74)	Double kick	(p. 80)
Side kick	(p. 76)	Speed kick drill	(p. 81)
Roundhouse kick	(p. 77)	Step kick	(p. 79)
Crescent kicks	(p. 75)	Back kick	(p. 77)

Elbow strikes

Forward	(p. 82)	Downward	(p. 83)
Reverse	(p. 82)	Side	(p. 84)
Upward	(p. 83)		

(continued)

KARATE WORKOUT: TOURNAMENT SEASON

INTERMEDIATE (continued)

Knee strikes

Straight knee	(p. 84)	Elbow and knee speed drill	(p. 85)
Roundhouse knee	(p. 85)		

Takedowns, throws, and sweeps

Shoulder takedown	(p. 87)	Hip throw	(p. 89)
Elbow takedown	(p. 88)	Takedown countering roundhouse kick	(p. 90)

Blocks

Downward block	(p. 91)	Blocking drill	(p. 94)
Upper block	(p. 91)	Foot and leg blocks	(p. 93)
Crescent blocks	(p. 92)		

DEFENSIVE MANEUVERS (5 MIN.)

Body shifting drill	(p. 94)	Footwork drills	(p. 95)
Footwork practice	(p. 95)		

TIMING TECHNIQUES (5-10 MIN.)

Reverse kick against side kick	(p. 139)	Spinning wheel kick against	
Reverse kick against reverse kick	(p. 140)	spinning wheel kick	(p. 142)
Reverse kick against roundhouse kick	(p. 141)		

ADVANCED COMBINATION DRILL (VARIATION 1, 5 MIN.) (P. 143)

BOXING TECHNIQUES (2-MIN. ROUNDS AGAINST A HEAVY BAG)

Punch combinations	(p. 148)
Bob-and-weave	(p. 149)

STEP SPARRING (5-10 MIN.)

Counter with hand techniques;
  add front kick
	(p. 101)	Counter with double kick; add front
		  kick; add middle-high double kick
			(p. 102)

Counter with hand strike and elbow strike; add knee strike	(p. 101)		

INFORMAL SPARRING PRACTICE (10-20 MIN.)

Heavy bag/shadow spar if no partner (p. 103)

COOL-DOWN

Focused breathing (1 min.)	(p. 117)
Visualization (3 min.)	(p. 117)

KARATE WORKOUT: TOURNAMENT SEASON

ADVANCED

Duration: Workout should last about an hour per session, six days per week.

Alternate the Conditioning Plan with the Sparring Plan. Monday, Wednesday, and Friday should be devoted to conditioning, with Tuesday, Thursday, and Saturday devoted to sparring.

CONDITIONING PLAN

WARM-UP (5 MIN.)

Treadmill	(p. 121)
Jump rope	(p. 122)

STRETCHES (5-10 MIN.)

Neck stretch	(p. 122)	Open stretch	(p. 123)
Shoulder stretch	(p. 122)	Bicycle stretch	(p. 124)
Wrist stretch	(p. 122)	Hamstring stretch	(p. 124)
Back stretch	(p. 123)	Quadriceps stretch	(p. 124)
Hip flexor stretch	(p. 123)	Calf raises	(p. 124)
Groin stretch	(p. 123)		

STRENGTH TRAINING AND CONDITIONING (20-30 MIN.)

Weightlifting, if desired	(p. 125)	Push-ups (15×)	(p. 128)
Crunches (15×)	(p. 127)	Push-up variations 1, 2, and 3	
Crunch variations 1, 2, 3, and 4		(15× each)	(p. 128)
(15× each)	(p. 127)	Pull-ups (5 without spotter)	(p. 128)
Boxer sit-ups (30×)	(p. 127)	Slow motion kicks (30 sec. for each	
Rope-ups (30×)	(p. 128)	technique)	(p. 129)

FLEXIBILITY (5-10 MIN.)

Hamstring lift, with partner	(p. 130)	Chambering drill (all kicks,	
Groin lift, with partner	(p. 130)	5× each leg, waist high)	(p. 130)

SPEED (5-10 MIN.)

Frog jumps (45 sec.)	(p. 131)	Hand response drill	
Jumping drill (knee high, 15×,		(1-2 in. or 3-5 cm)	(p. 133)
no mistakes)	(p. 131)	Kick response drill	
Sweeping drill (knee high, 15×,		(continue for 90 sec.)	(p. 133)
no mistakes)	(p. 132)	Kick response variation (10×)	(p. 133)
Punching drill			
(60 punches in 30 sec.)	(p. 132)		

(continued)

SPARRING PLAN

WARM-UP (5 MIN.)

Treadmill	(p. 121)
Jump rope	(p. 122)

STRETCHES (5 MIN.)

Neck stretch	(p. 122)	Open stretch	(p. 123)
Shoulder stretch	(p. 122)	Bicycle stretch	(p. 124)
Wrist stretch	(p. 122)	Hamstring stretch	(p. 124)
Back stretch	(p. 123)	Quadriceps stretch	(p. 124)
Hip flexor stretch	(p. 123)	Calf raises	(p. 124)
Groin stretch	(p. 123)		

TECHNIQUES PRACTICE (USING HEAVY BAG OR TARGET, 10-15 MIN.)

Punches

Forefist	(p. 65)	Double punch	(p. 67)
Straight punch	(p. 66)	Striking post drill	(p. 71)
Reverse punch	(p. 66)	Step-and-punch drill	(p. 73)

Hand Strikes

Knife hand strike	(p. 67)	Backfist	(p. 70)
Ridge hand strike	(p. 68)	Downward hammer fist strike	(p. 70)
Reverse ridge hand strike	(p. 69)	Horizontal hammer fist strike	(p. 71)
Palm strike	(p. 69)	Double hand strike	(p. 67)

Kicks

Front kick	(p. 74)	Speed kick drill	(p. 81)
Side kick	(p. 76)	Step kick	(p. 79)
Roundhouse kick	(p. 77)	Back kick	(p. 77)
Crescent kicks	(p. 75)	Jumping kicks	(p. 78)
Double kick	(p. 80)		

KARATE WORKOUT: TOURNAMENT SEASON
ADVANCED *(continued)*

Elbow strikes

Forward	(p. 82)	Downward	(p. 83)
Reverse	(p. 82)	Side	(p. 84)
Upward	(p. 83)		

Knee strikes

Straight-knee	(p. 84)	Elbow and knee speed drill	(p. 85)
Roundhouse knee	(p. 85)		

Takedowns, throws, and sweeps

Shoulder takedown	(p. 87)	Hip throw	(p. 89)
Elbow takedown	(p. 88)	Takedown countering roundhouse kick	(p. 90)

Blocks

Downward block	(p. 91)	Blocking drill	(p. 94)
Upper block	(p. 92)	Foot and leg blocks	(p. 93)
Crescent blocks	(p. 92)		

DEFENSIVE MANEUVERS (5 MIN.)

Body shifting drill	(p. 94)	Footwork drills	(p. 95)
Footwork practice	(p. 95)		

TIMING TECHNIQUES (5-10 MIN.)

Reverse kick against side kick	(p. 139)	Spinning wheel kick against	
Reverse kick against reverse kick	(p. 140)	spinning wheel kick	(p. 142)
Reverse kick against roundhouse kick	(p. 141)		

ADVANCED COMBINATION DRILL (VARIATION 1 , 5 MIN.) (P. 143)

BOXING TECHNIQUES (2-MIN. ROUNDS AGAINST A HEAVY BAG)

Punch combinations	(p. 148)
Bob-and-weave	(p. 149)

STEP SPARRING (5-10 MIN.)

Create own step sparring sequences (p. 100)

INFORMAL SPARRING PRACTICE (10-20 MIN.)

Heavy bag/shadow spar if no partner   (p. 103)

COOL-DOWN

Focused breathing (1 min.)	(p. 117)
Visualization (3 min.)	(p. 117)

Workout Log

Warm-up <u>Jump Rope</u> _____ 5 minutes

Stretches

<u>Neck stretch – all directions</u> _____ time <u>10 sec.</u> reps <u>5</u>

_____ time _____ reps _____

_____ time _____ reps _____

_____ time _____ reps _____

Strength Training and Conditioning

Lifts (optional)

_____ reps _____ sets _____ weight _____

_____ reps _____ sets _____ weight _____

_____ reps _____ sets _____ weight _____

_____ reps _____ sets _____ weight _____

Isometrics (crunches, push-ups, etc.)

_____ reps _____

_____ reps _____

_____ reps _____

_____ reps _____

Slow motion kicks

_____ time _____

_____ time _____

_____ time _____

_____ time _____

Flexibility Exercises

_____ time _____ reps _____

_____ time _____ reps _____

_____ time _____ reps _____

_____ time _____ reps _____

Workout Log *(continued)*

Speed Drills

_____ time _____ reps _____

_____ time _____ reps _____

_____ time _____ reps _____

_____ time _____ reps _____

Techniques Practice

_____ reps/time _____

_____ reps/time _____

_____ reps/time _____

_____ reps/time _____

Body Shifting/Footwork: time _____

Timing Techniques

_____ reps/time _____

_____ reps/time _____

_____ reps/time _____

_____ reps/time _____

Combination Drills

_____ time _____

Step Sparring

_____ reps/time _____

_____ reps/time _____

_____ reps/time _____

Informal Sparring Practice: time _____

Formal Sparring Practice: time _____

Comments

_____

_____

SUGGESTED READINGS

Aaberg, Everett. 1998. *Muscle mechanics*. Champaign, IL: Human Kinetics.

Cho, Sihak Henry. 1968. *Korean Karate: Free Fighting Techniques*. Rutland, VT: Charles E. Tuttle and Company.

Hickey, Patrick M. 1997. *Karate: Techniques and Tactics*. Champaign, IL: Human Kinetics.

Lawler, Jennifer. 1998. *Martial Arts for Women: A Practical Guide*. Wethersfield, CT: Turtle Press.

—. 1998. *Secrets of Taekwondo*. Chicago: NTC/Contemporary.

—. 1998. *Weight Training for Martial Artists*. Wethersfield, CT: Turtle Press.

Moeller, Mark. 1995. *Karate-do Foundations*. Indianapolis: Masters Press.

Park, Yeon Hwan, and Tom Seabourne. 1997. *Taekwondo: Techniques and Tactics*. Champaign, IL: Human Kinetics.

INDEX

ABOUT THE AUTHORS

Grandmaster Woo Jin Jung is a lifelong Taekwondo artist who has attained eighth *dan* black belt status. Master Jung cofounded—with Chuck Norris—the Martial Arts Federation for World Peace. Throughout a teaching career that spans 35 years, he has trained thousands of martial artists, including many premier practitioners and instructors. Master Jung's Taekwondo headquarters is based in Cedar Rapids, Iowa, and branch schools are located throughout the Midwest. He is vice president of Tri-Mount Publications, publishers of *Tae Kwon Do Times*. Master Jung lives in Cedar Rapids.

Jennifer Lawler, a freelance writer and black belt martial artist, earned her PhD in English from the University of Kansas. She has played a pivotal role in the development, organization, and explanation of Master Jung's profound insight. An accomplished author, she has written 14 books, including *The Martial Arts Encyclopedia*, *Martial Arts for Women: A Practical Guide*, *Weight Training for Martial Artists*, and *The Secrets of Tae Kwon Do*. She has trained for seven years in Taekwondo and holds a second degree black belt. Lawler lives in Lawrence, Kansas.

Pursue excellence *and*
Enhance performance

Embracing Your Potential

The drive to be #1 in a professional field or on a playing field is a powerful source of motivation for many people. Others place a higher priority on becoming a better person. *Embracing Your Potential* explains how to achieve excellence and balance in both the performance and personal domains of life.

Both inspirational and practical, *Embracing Your Potential* shares insights and quotes from elite athletes, performers, and people in highly demanding jobs. It also features 30 exercises that can help readers make meaningful, lasting changes to boost their performance and enrich their lives.

1998 • Paperback • 208 pp • Item PORL0831
ISBN 0-88011-831-8 • $15.95 ($22.95 Canadian)

High-Powered Plyometrics

Enter *High-Powered Plyometrics*—the most advanced, comprehensive guide to explosive power training for athletes, coaches, and conditioning experts. The book covers it all, from the principles of high-intensity plyometric training to the development of long- and short-term training programs for 21 sports. More than 360 photos illustrate 77 exercises to increase lower-, middle-, and upper-body power. Exercise descriptions and intensity guidelines provide step-by-step instructions to ensure correct technique and proper workload.

1999 • Paperback • 232 pp • Item PRAD0784
ISBN 0-88011-784-2 • $19.95 ($29.95 Canadian)

Power Eating

Never has there been a book like this! Even for those who've never given diet a second thought, *Power Eating* makes it easy to build a body that's fit for the ring—and do it safely, healthily, and legally.

Authored by one of the first sports nutrition scientists to take a serious look at nutrition and strength training, *Power Eating* is loaded with the latest findings in the field—including new data on supplements and ergogenic aids. No other credible source provides the research-based information presented here.

1998 • Paperback • 240 pp • Item PKLE0702
ISBN 0-88011-702-8 • $15.95 ($23.95 Canadian)

To place orders, U.S. customers call
TOLL FREE 1-800-747-4457
Customers outside the U.S.: place your order using the appropriate telephone number/address shown in the front of this book.

HUMAN KINETICS
The Premier Publisher for Sports & Fitness
P.O. Box 5076, Champaign, IL 61825-5076

www.humankinetics.com